What to Say
When You Don't Know What to Say

H. NORMAN WRIGHT

HARVEST HOUSE PUBLISHERS
EUGENE, OREGON

Cover photo © mythja / Shutterstock

Cover by Dugan Design Group, Bloomington, Minnesota

WHAT TO SAY WHEN YOU DON'T KNOW WHAT TO SAY
Copyright © 2014 H. Norman Wright
Published by Harvest House Publishers
Eugene, Oregon 97402
www.harvesthousepublishers.com

Library of Congress Cataloging-in-Publication Data
Wright, H. Norman.
What to say when you don't know what to say / H. Norman Wright.
    pages cm
ISBN 978-0-7369-5847-9 (pbk.)
ISBN 978-0-7369-5848-6 (eBook)
    1. Church work with the bereaved. 2. Friendship—Religious aspects—Christianity. 3. Interpersonal relations—Religious aspects—Christianity. 4. Consolation. 5. Communication—Religious aspects—Christianity. I. Title.
BV4460.W75 2014
248.8'6—dc23

2013048429

Printed in the United States of America

14 15 16 17 18 19 20 21 22 / VP-JH / 10 9 8 7 6 5 4 3 2 1

Contents

You *Can* Help 5

1. Called to Help. 9
2. Don't Be a Miserable Comforter 25
3. If You Want to Help, Listen 41
4. Understanding What Your Friend Is Experiencing 55
5. Understanding a Friend in Crisis. 73
6. Loss or Trauma?. 89
7. The Hazards of Trauma. 97
8. Helping Your Friend 111
9. When Depression Hits 121
10. Helping a Suicidal Friend 133
11. Say It in Writing 151
12. Praying for Your Friend 167
13. What to Do and What Not to Do. 179
14. When to Make a Referral 193

Notes 197

Charts

Phases of Bereavement Intensity 67
Phases of a Crisis 77
Ball of Grief. 81
Recovery Time Line 107

You *Can* Help

In one small European village was a town square that held a special statue. This statue was the pride and joy of the residents, but World War II arrived, and soon the bombs began falling on the town. One day the statue was hit and blown to pieces. The residents collected all the shattered pieces and slowly did what they could to rebuild it. When they finished the reconstruction of their beloved statue of Jesus, they noticed that the only pieces missing were the hands. So they placed a plaque at the base of the statue with these words: *Now we are the only hands that Jesus has.*

Isn't this our calling to those around us? We are Jesus' hands, as the apostle Paul told the Christians in Corinth: "Praise be to the God and Father of our Lord Jesus Christ, the Father of compassion and the God of all comfort, who comforts us in all our troubles, so that *we can comfort those in any trouble* with the comfort we ourselves receive from God" (2 Corinthians 1:3-4).

Many years ago (more than I'd like to admit), I was serving as minister of education and youth. A man by the name of Alan Loy McGinnis attended our church while completing his graduate work. Since he was also a minister, he would preach from time to time in the evening services. One Sunday night he walked up to the pulpit and said, "Tonight I would like to share with you what to say, what not to say, what to do, and what not to do at a time of bereavement."

Ours was not a note-taking congregation—until that moment. As I sat on the platform I could see people reaching for offering envelopes, prayer requests cards, or any other piece of paper they could find to write on. I still have my notes from that evening. It was the first (and unfortunately the last) time I've ever heard a message on how to help another person at a time of need. Those in attendance that evening left with a greater sense of confidence on how to help people.

Yes, we'll be more likely to reach out if we know what to say. And yes, helping a hurting person can be a bit scary. So if we have the desire to reach out and help, why do we hesitate? Because we grapple with questions like "What do I say?" "What do I do?" "What should I avoid?" We want to do the right thing and say what will help, but we're not sure what will accomplish that.

That's where *What to Say When You Don't Know What to Say* comes in! This easy-to-read book offers the knowledge, wisdom, and resources you need to confidently and competently help family, friends, and acquaintances when they need comfort and support.

Help for You as Caregiver

Before becoming significantly involved in helping others, you need to be aware of a problem that none of us are immune to. It has different names, including *compassion fatigue, helper shutdown,* or *helper burnout,* and it can happen to doctors, nurses, counselors, rescue workers, and anyone involved in helping others. It seems to be a case of emotional contagion—you end up catching the disorder of the person you're helping. You become emotionally drained by caring too much. It's stress from wanting to help another person. When you minister to a friend, he may leave feeling better, but now you're absorbed in his problems emotionally as well as mentally.

This can happen for several reasons. It can be an overload if you're helping a number of hurting individuals at the same time. The desire to help others is good, but you need to realize not everyone will be helped and there are some who aren't willing to take the necessary steps to change. Some helpers end up with "mission failure" or they say, "I didn't help them enough." This won't happen to you. The Person bringing the changes about will be the Lord. So as you help, you also need to relinquish your friend to Jesus' care and attention. Your value in helping others is to be there for them. You'll be a more effective helper when you follow the helpful guidelines in this book, but don't evaluate your success based on how well the person you're helping responds. As a professional counselor for many years, I learned that sometimes helpers don't get to see the results of our efforts as people move on. If you are too empathetic and feel what your friend is feeling too much, you will begin to carry his burdens around. That's not your job. Remember, the person you're helping is in God's hands, not yours.

If you have unresolved trauma in your life, be prepared to have it activated when you work with someone who has experienced trauma. What you hear may hit close to home.

What will especially impact you is helping children who have experienced trauma. This happens to even the most experienced professional helpers.

What can you do? Make sure you maintain balance in your life. You need to allow time for tending to and nurturing yourself through the Word, healthy friendships, exercise, recreation, devotional reading, and laughter. You need to allow others to care for you too.

Sometimes you discover that helping certain friends is too draining. You feel empty after every encounter. Your friend may need assistance from someone other than you. Be aware of your thoughts. If you're constantly thinking about your friend's problems and you don't relinquish his issues to the Lord, you could end up in difficulties yourself. Two resources you may want to read and recommend to those you help are my books *Making Peace with Your Past* and *A Better Way to Think*.

Despite these risks, helping people is a God-given calling that provides many opportunities for you to comfort and enrich the lives of those around you. When you actively participate with Him in this way, you too will be incredibly blessed.

Chapter 1

Called to Help

When a family member or friend tells you about a difficult life situation, a tragic accident, or even a life-threatening illness, you want to help. You want to reach out and offer comfort and support. Sadly, how to best do that is an area not taught very often. And even when there are articles or classes on providing compassion, they're usually cursory and unhelpful when it comes to real-life situations.

You're not alone in your concern of how to help others. I know you don't want to say or do the wrong thing and inadvertently hurt the people who come to you for help. And during a loss or crisis, you can't really rely on them to tell you what they really need. They may not know or they may not have the energy it takes to tell you.

What can you say or do when someone comes to you...

- "I've just been told I have cancer...and it's terminal."

- "I just got a phone call. He's dead...he's been killed...my husband."

- "My daughter just told me she's been molested for three years."

- "I was in the grocery store, and it was robbed. The gun went off. I can't even think right now."

- "I went to school to pick up my son, and he wasn't there. They told me he was kidnapped!"

- "My husband just told me he wants a divorce. I'm shocked. I didn't know anything was wrong."

One day I was sitting at the kitchen table in my daughter's home looking through a magazine while she fed her six-month-old daughter. The phone rang and Sheryl answered the call while continuing to feed her daughter. When she said, "Oh no. I'm so sorry to hear that. That must have been a shock," my ears perked up. Being a counselor, I was intrigued so I continued to listen. It was apparent that her friend was in some kind of distress. I observed Sheryl while she listened and reflected back what she was hearing. She made statements like, "So you found the evidence, and that's what led you to confront him" and "You're sounding hurt and disappointed." From time to time she asked questions: "Are any of your children aware of this?" and "How will she handle this at her stage in life?" She also asked, "Had you thought about this possibility?" and "Have you considered this?"

When her friend wasn't sure or seemed to waver, Sheryl asked, "Is that really your responsibility at this time…or is it his?" She was helping her friend consider the best things to do and encouraging her to take the necessary steps. "You've given him more than a chance and trusted his word. Now it's been broken. I think you know what to do." Then she helped her friend explore several options as well as the possible consequences. On several occasions she reflected and clarified while her friend was thinking out loud. I could tell just from my daughter's comments and expressions that her friend was devastated. I thought it was great that this caller had a trusted friend to talk to and help her work through this life-changing event.

My daughter wasn't judgmental in any way as she assisted her friend in clarifying the problem. Her friend needed someone to give her support, someone to listen, someone to help her sort through the options, and someone to help her stabilize her life at that time. After Sheryl hung up, we talked about the situation for a while.

Sheryl made the comment, "I'm sure glad I'm not a counselor. I wouldn't want to do this for a living." I just looked at her, smiled, and said, "Oh sure. You've only done this for 15 years as a manicurist. You've helped as many women as some counselors have while you were sitting there doing their nails." She laughed because it was true. She's helped many people who would never go to a professional counselor or a pastor. But her clients listened to Sheryl because of her listening ability, her insights, her experiences, and her desire to help. And people will listen to you too.

After more than forty years of being a counselor, I'm convinced that as many as one-third to one-half of all the people I've seen didn't need to see me. That is, they wouldn't have needed to see me if they'd had a trained pastor, lay caregiver, or knowledgeable friend to meet with. I'm all for professional counseling when it's needed, but many issues can be resolved with the help of a friend who has learned the simple skills to help others. And, as Christians, ministering to people is part of our calling! Unfortunately, many people back off from this aspect because they don't know what to say or do. That's understandable, and I'm glad you want to solve that problem. Even as a long-time counselor I sometimes come across an issue I'm not sure how to handle. When that happens I do some research and talk to people to learn what I need so I can help.

When it comes to helping people, there's more to it than just feeling comfortable talking and being knowledgeable about the particular subject involved. You need to understand that your friend—the person you're helping—is probably not quite himself. He's different. His thinking is affected. His behavior might be erratic. His emotions are probably off the scale. So how can you help your friend get back to normal? The primary requirement is caring. Harold Smith described the process so well:

> Grief sharers always look for an opportunity to actively care. You can never "fix" an individual's grief, but you can wash the sink full of dishes, listen to him or her talk, take his or her kids to the park. You can never "fix" an individual's grief, but you can visit the cemetery with him or her.
>
> Grief sharing is not about fixing—it's about showing up. Coming alongside. Being interruptible. "Hanging out" with the bereaving. In the words of World War II veterans, "present and reporting for duty."
>
> The grief path is not a brief path. It's a marathon, not a sprint.[1]

What can you expect from a friend who is hurting? Actually, not very much. And the more his experience moves beyond loss and closer to crisis or trauma, the more this is true. Sometimes you'll see a friend experiencing a case of the "crazies." His responses seem irrational. He's not himself. His behavior is different from or even abnormal compared to a person not going through a major loss. Just remember he's reacting to an out-of-the-ordinary event. What he *experienced* is abnormal, so his *response* is actually quite normal. If what the person has experienced is traumatic, he may even exhibit some of the symptoms of Attention Deficit Disorder (ADD).

These are responses you *can* expect. Your friend is no longer functioning as he once did—and probably won't for a while. And just because your friend is this way, he is *not* to be avoided. He needs you at this time. He needs friends to support and encourage him.

You Are Needed!

When a person experiences a sudden intrusion or disruption in her life, you are needed. If you or other friends aren't available, the only person she has to talk with for guidance, support, and direction is herself. And who wants support from someone struggling with a case of the "crazies"?

A problem may arise if your friend doesn't realize that she needs you…or doesn't realize she needs you at this *particular time*. Your sensitivity is needed at this point. Remember, when your friend is hurting and facing a loss, you too are dealing with a loss. The relationship you had with your friend has changed. It's not the same. It's no longer equal. You may feel as though you're the giver and your friend is the taker. Your relationship is off balance. The sharing the two of you had before has changed. The give-and-take you used to experience has vanished. What's important to you doesn't seem as important to your friend right now. Your life and experiences have taken a backseat to the present experiences of your friend.

> Your friend in mourning—though he doesn't perceive himself that way—is self-centered. You simply cannot exist for

him as a whole person, probably for a very long time. This can be hard on relationships. Friends get weary of ceasing to be perceived as human beings with feelings and problems and hopes in their own right. They get weary of being there for the other person in seemingly a one-sided relationship. But suffice it to say that your friend in mourning will not be able to empathize with you about things involving you for many months—or maybe years.[2]

And that's okay even though it can be difficult. You can't put a time limit on your role as a helper or giver. This may get old for you, especially when it stretches on for months. And remember that when your relationship gets back to normal, it will be a "new" normal. It won't be the same. Sometimes a hurting friend ends up feeling resentful over being dependent on you while at the same time appreciating all you've done for her. And sometime your friend may do the same for you.

What Can You Do Right Now?

You can listen even when your friend isn't talking. Sometimes she's not able to talk, but your attentive presence lets her know you're ready to listen. Let her know you want to hear her story when she's up to talking about it.

If your friend is devastated and coming apart at the seams or sitting there stunned, you can't make her feel better or "fix" her or the situation. When you try, it's often to help you feel useful and relieve your anxiety of seeing someone in this state. We all tend to do that. Remember, you can never be all you want to be or all your friend wants you to be for her.[3]

What else can you expect? The world your friend experiences now won't be your world. Often she will retreat into her world and not let you in. Because of what she's going through, your activities may not seem as significant as they once did. You may reevaluate your own standards and values. Your family may see how your friend's problems are changing you, and they may pressure you to back away from her. They want *you* back to normal.

Yes, you will be hurt at times since some of what you offer or do for your friend will be rejected. Because you haven't experienced the same loss, she may feel uncomfortable with you—while at the same time she wants and asks for your help. Remember, your friend is not functioning normally. In your heart and mind, give her permission not to be as she was. If something is said or she didn't respond how you expected, you may wonder, "Did I say something wrong? Am I off base?" The answer is no. You're dealing with her unpredictability in the midst of her crisis. *You* are all right and doing fine.

> Reassure your friend that what he or she is experiencing is normal and natural.

You may be tempted at times to set your friend straight spiritually. You might hear her say, "I thought I could count on God, but even He let me down" or "How could a loving God let something like that happen?" You may even hear, "I think I'm losing my faith in God. I can't even pray anymore." Squelch your desire to quote Bible verses, recommend a specific spiritual book, or offer answers for why she may be interpreting the situation that way. Instead, be glad she's sharing where she is spiritually. Respond with simple expressions of support: "Yes, what's happened doesn't make much sense, does it? It's hard to understand. I wish I had an answer for you." Or you can just listen and reflect back to her what you're hearing.

There will be times when your friend doesn't want you around. If you sense that might be the case, ask, "What would be more comfortable for you at this time—for me to be here with you or for me to give you some space? I can do either." Let your friend know that you won't be offended if she doesn't want you there. If your presence isn't needed, gently say, "I'll check back with you another time to see what I can do to assist you," and then quietly leave. She is not rejecting you. She's dealing with her crisis the best she can and just needs some space.

And since no one is a mind reader, there will be times when you don't have any idea what your friend needs. Let her know it's all right for her to tell you specifically, even if it's just saying, "I don't know."

You're going to read this next statement several times in this book because of its importance: *The best support you can give your friend is to normalize her feelings.* This simply means reassuring her that what she is experiencing is normal and natural. She isn't crazy, and she isn't going crazy. This assurance may provide the greatest relief of all. To give it, however, means *you* need to understand what someone usually experiences from loss or trauma. (We'll discuss trauma specifically in chapters 6 and 7.)

Biblical Wisdom for Helping

How can you help a friend? There are many elements involved. Proverbs 3:5-6 instructs us to "lean on, trust in, and be confident in the Lord with all your heart and mind and do not rely on your own insight or understanding. In all your ways know, recognize, and acknowledge Him, and He will direct and make straight and plain your paths" (AMP). A similar thought is found in Proverbs 15:28: "The mind of the [uncompromisingly] righteous studies how to answer, but the mouth of the wicked pours out evil things" (AMP, brackets in original).

> Helping others includes experiencing genuine interest and love for them.

Even with all their years of training and experience, professional counselors frequently wonder what they should do or say. This experience prompts all of us to go "back to the need." You'll find yourself there time and time again. If you assist your friend out of your own strength, mistakes will be made. We all need to rely on the power and wisdom of God.

Helping others includes experiencing genuine interest and love for them. You can rely on the power of God for that love. If it's not there, you can't fake it. Your friends will know if you are. "Oil and perfume rejoice the heart; so does the sweetness of a friend's counsel that comes from the heart" (Proverbs 27:9 AMP). It's so easy to toss off an answer or response that's superficial, but it won't meet your friend's need. And because it doesn't deal with the problem she'll be disappointed. Ask yourself, "How do I really feel about this person who needs help? Am I genuinely concerned?" If you aren't, pray about the situation and your attitude. Perhaps you're not the one supposed to help. You'll be drawn to help some and not others. It could be their problems are beyond you, overwhelm you, or activate unresolved issues in your life.

Communicating Gently

To help someone, you need to know when to speak and when enough has been said:

> In a multitude of words transgression is not lacking, but he who restrains his lips is prudent (Proverbs 10:19 AMP).

> Don't talk so much. You keep putting your foot in your mouth. Be sensible and turn off the flow! (10:19 TLB).

> He who belittles and despises his neighbor lacks sense, but a man of understanding keeps silent (Proverbs 11:12 AMP).

> The smart person says very little, and one with understanding stays calm (Proverbs 17:27 NCV).

> Even fools seem to be wise if they keep quiet; if they don't speak, they appear to understand (17:28 NCV).

> Do you see a man who is hasty in his words? There is more hope for a [self-confident] fool than for him (29:20 AMP, brackets in original).

Being hasty means you blurt out what you're thinking without considering the effect it might have on others. If you're an extrovert, you probably need to talk while thinking something through. Extroverts tend to speak first and then realize what they've said later. When you're ministering to a hurting friend and he shares something that shocks you, don't feel you have to respond immediately. This might be a time to hold back and get your thoughts in order. I've heard people say, "You did *what?*" in response to someone, and it immediately shut down communication. Instead, take a few moments to pray and ask God to give you the best words. Then formulate what you want to say carefully.

You could say, "Give me some time to respond to that" or "I need a few minutes to go through what you said." This takes the pressure off you and your friend.

Another passage that reflects the idea of understanding is Proverbs 25:20 (NCV): "Singing songs to someone who is sad is like taking away his coat on a cold day or pouring vinegar on soda." Being joyful, making sarcastic comments, telling jokes, or making statements like "Snap out of it" are inappropriate when someone is deeply hurting and suffering. Your friend needs to know that being emotional in difficult situations is normal, and you're okay with it.

If you don't know what to say, one of the best things to do is *ask for information*: "Tell me more about it" or "What are you thinking about this?"

Timing is yet another important communication consideration. "A man has joy making an apt answer, and a word spoken at the right moment—how good it is!" (Proverbs 15:23 AMP). A wise response or answer needs to be spoken at the right moment to be heard and accepted. "A word fitly spoken and in due season is like apples of gold in settings of silver" (Proverbs 25:11 AMP).

Being Discreet but Thinking Safety

Keeping confidences is foundational to helping people. Do you keep a confidence when a friend shares something with you? This adage applies to your friend as well as to you: "Gossips can't keep secrets, so avoid people who talk too much" (Proverbs 20:19 NCV). "Gossips can't keep secrets, but a trustworthy person can" (11:13 NCV). Undoubtedly most of us have had the temptation to share an interesting tidbit about someone with others. Yes, even confidences from friends. And the more shocking it is, the more we're tempted to share. But such conversation is a violation of trust and friendship. Tremendous damage can be done, especially when your friend is in such a vulnerable state. "He who guards his mouth and his tongue keeps himself from troubles" (Proverbs 21:23 AMP). So when you're told sensitive information, use your best judgment about confidentiality. Ask God to help you bury confidential information deep inside or you can give it to the Lord and let it go so it won't be on the tip of your tongue. Remember, your friend is in an emotional state and might not guard what she says as much as she usually would. If you're unsure, ask your friend whether the information is okay to share with her family or other friends.

There are some circumstances and situations that cancel the usual confidentiality principles. If your friend is self-harming, suicidal, or threatening harm to someone else, get immediate help and make sure everyone stays safe.

Offering Advice

On many occasions all of us have struggled and friends have given us advice—some good, some not so good. And sometimes the advice was good but not what we needed at that time. In fact, it's possible we could receive five different viewpoints if we asked five different people. Then we're left wondering, *What do I do now? Whose advice should I follow?*

If you have suggestions for someone struggling, give them in tentative form so the person can choose or have input. "What if you did…?" "Have you considered…?" "What possibilities have you come up with?" A safety factor you can employ if you're going to give advice is to give several alternatives. Don't say to a person, "This is what you need to do." If you do that, you assume responsibility for the solution and outcome, and if your suggestion doesn't work, the person may come back and say, "You really gave me stupid advice. It didn't work, and made things worse. It's your fault." Offering several suggestions in a tentative way not only is safer for you, but it also helps your friend think through the scenarios better. Most people have the ability to resolve their problems, but they often need the encouragement to do so.

Considering Confrontation

One of the ways of helping a friend is gentle confrontation when you see him heading down the wrong path. Confrontation is not attacking the person. He may already be feeling guilty and ashamed so for him to experience judgment or condemnation rather than a gentle nudge seems like nothing less than rejection.

Confronting another person should only be considered when you've experienced empathy for the person. "Confrontation" is an *act of grace*. It's done to reveal discrepancies or distortions in someone's intended direction or thinking. Confrontation is also used to challenge and strengthen underdeveloped and unused skills and resources of your friend.

Your purpose in confronting your friend is to help him make better decisions for himself, become more accepting of where he is in life, and be less destructive and more productive. "Wounds from a friend can be trusted, but an enemy multiplies kisses" (Proverbs 27:6). "A rebuke impresses a discerning person more than a hundred lashes a fool" (Proverbs 17:10).

Remember, you can't use the same approach for every person. You need to be sensitive to the person's needs and personality. Your adaptability is important. "We earnestly beseech you, brethren, admonish (warn and seriously advise) those who are out of line...*encourage the timid and fainthearted, help and give your support to the weak souls*, [and] *be very patient* with everybody [always keeping your temper]" (1 Thessalonians 5:14 AMP, brackets in original).

How do you confront with grace? Not with anger or with a statement that casts judgment. You may want to point out that what someone is doing is irresponsible or even dumb, but you'll offend and even sever the relationship by doing that. Your friend needs to hear care and concern in your voice. Confrontation should be done in a soft manner with statements such as, "I wonder if..." "Could it be...?" "Is it possible...?" "Does this make sense to you?" and "How do you react to this perception?" Using questions, lead the person to what you want him to consider. Practice asking the questions out loud again and again until they're a comfortable part of your helping reservoir of wise approaches.

Offering Help and Hope

Another principle we find in the Word of God is helping and edifying. Some of these passages might be familiar to you. "Carry each other's burdens, and in this way you will fulfill the law of Christ" (Galatians 6:2). "Let us then definitely aim for and eagerly pursue what makes for harmony and for mutual upbuilding (edification and development) of one another" (Romans 14:19 AMP). The word *edify*, which is part of helping, means "to hold up or to promote growth in Christian wisdom, grace, virtue, and holiness." Helping includes edification. Helping means "assisting a person to do something for her betterment." Ask yourself, "Is what I'm sharing with that person going to cause her to grow in Christ and assist her to be strong?" A friend might come to you and say, "I really want you to help me." What does she mean by *help*? She might mean agreeing with her point of view or even taking her side. That is where you can get into difficulty. You want to avoid taking sides.

Another way of helping others is giving encouragement. "Anxiety in a man's heart weighs it down, but an encouraging word makes it glad" (Proverbs 12:25 AMP). "Encourage (admonish, exhort) one another and edify (strengthen and build up) one another, just as you are doing" (1 Thessalonians 5:11 AMP). The *American Heritage Dictionary* offers one of the better definitions of *encourage*: "tendency or disposition to expect the best possible outcome, or to dwell on the most hopeful aspect of a situation." When this is your attitude or perspective, you'll be able to encourage others. Encouragement is "to inspire; to continue on a chosen course; to impart courage or confidence." Encouragement is recognizing the other person as having worth and dignity. It means paying attention to her when she is sharing with you. It's listening to her in a way that lets her know she's being listened to. "When Apollos wanted to go to Achaia, the brothers and sisters *encouraged* him and wrote to the disciples there to welcome him" (Acts 18:27). The word *encourage* here means "to urge forward or persuade." In 1 Thessalonians 5:11, which I just shared with you, *encourage* means "to stimulate another person to the ordinary duties of life."

Scripture uses a variety of words to describe both our involvement with others as well as the actual relationship. *Urge* (Greek, *parakaleo*) means to "beseech or exhort." It is intended to create an environment of urgency to listen and respond to a directive. It is a mildly active verb Paul used: "I *urge* you, brothers and sisters, in view of God's mercy, to offer your bodies as a living sacrifice, holy and pleasing to God—this is your true and proper worship" (Romans 12:1) and "I always thank my God for you because of his grace given you in Christ Jesus" (1 Corinthians 1:4).

The word *encourage* (Greek, *paramutheomai*) means "to console, comfort, and cheer up." This process includes elements of understanding, redirecting thoughts, and a general shifting of focus from the negative to the positive. In the context of the verse, it refers to the timid individual who is discouraged and ready to give up. It's a matter of loaning your faith and hope to the person until her own develops.

Help (Greek, *anechomai*) primarily consists of "taking interest in, being devoted to, rendering assistance, or holding up spiritually and emotionally." It is not so much active involvement as a passive approach. It suggests the idea of coming alongside a person and supporting her. "We urge you, brothers and sisters, warn those who are idle and disruptive, encourage the disheartened, help the weak, be patient with everyone" (1 Thessalonians 5:14). In the context of that verse, *help* seems to refer to those who are incapable of helping themselves.

Hebrews 3:13 says we're to "encourage one another daily." In the setting of this verse, *encouragement* is associated with protecting a believer from callousness. Hebrews 10:25 refers to "encouraging one another." This time *encouraging* means to keep someone on her feet who, if left to herself, would collapse. Your encouragement serves like the concrete pilings of a structural support.

Involvement and empathy are the scriptural basis for helping, and empathy is one of the most important commodities for helping. It's viewing the situation through your friend's eyes and feeling as she feels. The scriptural admonition to bear one another's burdens and rejoice with those who rejoice and weep with those who weep reveals empathy (Galatians 6:2; Romans 12:15).

Empathy involves discrimination, the ability to distinguish through discernment how the other person is looking at the world. You want to get inside the other person and see the world through her perspective or frame of reference to get a feeling for what her world is like. You also want to communicate to your friend this understanding in such a manner that she realizes you have picked up on her feelings and, to some extent, her behavior. This is a learned skill. Be patient with yourself as you develop this ability. You want to see with your friend's eyes what her world is like. For instance, it's being able to see another person's joy, to understand what underlies that joy, and to communicate this understanding to the person. Can you do this? Yes!

One of my favorite true stories that describes how significant a person's presence can be in the life of another comes from a doctor:

> Barbara received another three courses of chemotherapy, but the tumor seemed to shrug off the drugs. The deposits grew in her liver and in her bones. She lost weight and spent most of the time in bed. After the last cycle of chemotherapy, I admitted her to the hospital with a high fever. Antibiotics stemmed an early bacterial infection.
>
> As Barbara slowly recovered from the infection, I told myself I knew of no drugs, either standard or experimental, that stood a real chance of ameliorating her condition. The time had come for me to tell her.
>
> I chose to visit in the early evening, when the hubbub of the hospital had settled down, so there would be less chance of distraction and interruption. Barbara greeted me warmly, as she always did. I moved a chair close to the bedside and grasped her hand. She returned the gesture, but it had little force. After we chatted for a short time about several articles in the day's newspaper, I began to break the bad news.
>
> "Barbara, we've known each other for well over a year, and we've been honest with each other every step of the way."
>
> Briefly, her lips trembled, and then she regained her composure. Her eyes told me she knew what I was about to say.
>
> "I know of no medicine that I can give at this point to help you."
>
> We sat in heavy silence.
>
> Barbara shook her head. "No, Jerry," she said. "You do have something to give. You have the medicine of friendship." [4]

Be open to God's leading at this time. May the words of a man who gave his life for others on September 11, 2001, at the World Trade Center guide you:

> Lord, take me where You want me to go,
> Let me meet whom You want me to meet.
> Help me to say what You want me to say.
> And keep me from getting in Your way![5]
>
> *Father Mychal Judge*

Chapter 2

Don't Be a Miserable Comforter

If an enemy were insulting me, I could endure it; if a foe were raising himself against me, I could hide. But it is you, a man like myself, my companion, my close friend, with whom I once enjoyed sweet fellowship at the house of God" (Psalm 55:12-14). "Even my close friend, someone I trusted, one who shared my bread, has turned against me" (Psalm 41:9).

There is one additional source of pain your friend will need to contend with—people who make statements that hurt rather than console, hinder rather than comfort, and prolong pain rather than relieve it. These people are "secondary wounders." They give unwanted and usually bad advice as well as improperly applied Scripture. These people are all around, including at church, and your friend won't be the first to experience this unfortunate phenomena. Remember Job from the Old Testament?

> [Job] had four well-meaning but insufferable friends who came over to cheer him up and try to explain [his suffering]. They said that anybody with enough sense to come in out of the rain knew that God was just. They said that anybody old enough to spell his own name knew that since God was just, he made bad things happen to bad people and good things happen to good people. They said that such being the case, you didn't need a Harvard diploma to figure out

that since bad things had happened to Job, then *ipso facto* he must have done something bad himself. But Job hadn't, and he said so, and that's not all he said either. "Worthless physicians are you all," he said. "Oh that you would keep silent, and it would be your wisdom" (Job 13:4-5). They were a bunch of theological quacks, in other words, and the smartest thing they could do was shut up. But they were too busy explaining things to listen.[1]

Words Better Left Unsaid

Expect people to make statements that your friend would rather not hear. It will be difficult for him to respond to these people the way he would like to because of his state of grief or trauma. Perhaps others would learn not to make such insensitive statements if someone spoke up and said, "That's not true, and it's not helpful. If you want to be helpful, I'd appreciate it if you would…" But sometimes we excuse what these people say as well meaning, which is questionable. Oftentimes they're just reflecting their own anxieties, fears, or lack of having dealt with issues in their lives. Remember, this is not advice coming from experts. It could also be that no one (including the church) has given them any assistance on what to say or do to be helpful.

Let your friend know he can anticipate at least three common reactions from the people he confides in.

The Inability of Others to Accept the Bad News

There are numerous reasons for the inability to accept bad news, but the results are the same: People can't handle the situation or accept the person who has created the problem. Often people will verbalize sympathy and support, but their attitudes and behaviors communicate rejection. Your hurting friend will wonder which message to believe. On one hand he'll find them reaching out to him, but on the other hand they're pulling away.

Remind him that when people are uncomfortable with a situation, they feel uncertain. By their nonverbal responses, they're saying, "I want you back to normal as soon as possible…or at least I want you to act that way." But your friend can't and won't be normal for some time, and no one else can determine how he should respond. This is *his* situation. He's upset over his tragedy and loss. No one should try to rob him of his feelings and grief. I read a statement once that describes death, but it applies to other situations as well: "When a person is born we celebrate; when they marry we jubilate; but when they die we act as if nothing happened."[2]

The more others hear about your friend's difficulties, the greater the level of their discomfort—and they don't want his discomfort invading their lives so they may distance themselves. I've seen situations in which the spouse, parents, or the children going through the difficulties were no longer invited to their friends' homes, as though what they were experiencing might be contagious.

When people react badly to your friend it may help if they explain some of the adjustments they're experiencing. If comfortable, the person who is hurting could tell others he understands how uncomfortable they may feel learning about his situation. He shouldn't expect them to open up and say they're having difficulty with the situation because they probably won't. But if he admits his struggle, along with his mixture of feelings, at least others may feel more comfortable around him, whether they admit anything or not.

Dealing with Unsolicited Advice

Everyone is an expert or knows of a similar case, and since those who care want to help, they give emphatic suggestions about steps that should be taken. Sometimes they're offended if your friend doesn't show enthusiasm and indicate he's going to follow their advice immediately. Too often, however, their suggestions are contrary to a selected plan or the advice of a counselor.

Advise your friend to thank these people for their concern and suggestions and let them know they're adding to the wealth of information he's gathering, but he shouldn't commit to taking their advice. There will likely be times when nothing is working, the experts don't know what to do, or he's in a state of panic and he may find himself jumping from one piece of advice to another. Soon he'll be overwhelmed by a lack of follow-through on any of the suggestions. Before he acts on suggestions, he needs to reflect on them. If he's still in a state of shock or crisis, he might need to let a few *trusted* friends help him make decisions.

Sometimes it's not just advice he has to contend with, but also the third degree. You've probably heard the questions like these before: "Has this happened before in your family?" "Do you have a good lawyer?"

Handling Too Much Help

Yet another reaction, especially from people who really care, will be to overwhelm your friend with help. I've seen relatives and friends invade a family's boundaries and take away their decision-making opportunities. Your friend needs help in determining how much assistance he wants and establishing boundaries with intrusive friends and relatives. Most people won't have any idea what he needs or doesn't need until your friend outlines it for them. They'll want to help, which is fine, but only your friend can determine the type of help he needs and wants. Remind him it's perfectly all right for him to be in charge of his decisions.

A good starting point for your friend is to make a list of his needs and questions, and then list the type of outside help he's looking for. It's all right to take time to think, to pray, and to consider the options and consequences of each. He doesn't need to let others pressure or rush him in to anything.[3]

What Not to Say

Listen to these firsthand experiences of being wounded by others.

> My first day back to work after my mother's funeral, a coworker said, "I know just how you feel. My cat died recently." How could someone compare my mother to a cat? It would have more sensitive to simply say, "I'm sorry."[4]

> Our young daughter, who was dying from leukemia, loved

to read. When we took her to the ophthalmologist for a new pair of glasses, he said, "She's going to die soon anyway. Don't waste your money on a new prescription." He didn't understand that dying children need to make every day count and live to the fullest the life they have left.[5]

My son, who had Down's syndrome, died when he was twenty years old. A relative said, "What a blessing. He is better off now." I wondered if her twenty-two-year-old son would be "better off" if he were dead and if that would bless her. Does an IQ make one life worth more than another? Does an IQ change a mother's grief? I had cared for my precious, loving son his entire life, and I desperately missed him and his daily hugs. Many thought I would be relieved. Very few people understood my loss and I felt very alone in my grieving.[6]

Following my miscarriage people would say, "At least you have other children" or "God probably took the baby because there was something wrong with it" or "At least you are healthy and will probably conceive again." After my grandfather died, my grandmother told me that friends said, "At least you had all those years together." Don't say *at least*. Don't try to minimize someone's pain. It only insults the griever.[7]

When my wife died, an acquaintance said, "God must have needed another angel in heaven, another flower in his garden." It is not comforting to have God reduced to a selfish, needy deity who must take from us. He is God.[8]

I waited for days, even weeks, before I could bring myself to tell anyone about our child. I used to think it wasn't because I was ashamed or embarrassed or anything, but I guess I did have those feelings. I don't know why I felt that way. Maybe I felt that John's rebellion was my fault, even though I knew it wasn't. It couldn't be. I guess I was afraid of their reaction. You never know what you're going to hear.

I didn't want their advice. They're not experts, and I didn't want them telling me we were bad parents.

Not only will there be comments that hurt, but responses such as withdrawing. Your friend may wonder if she's contracted the plague. One insightful individual said:

> You feel so isolated within yourself. When people withdraw from you because of their own discomfort, in a way, it's almost like an accusation that you were at fault. You feel you *must* have done something wrong, or this wouldn't be happening to you. On the other hand, you almost feel like they don't want to be around you because they feel it might be catching. I know people don't know what to say. I would rather they'd come and be with me or ask permission, "Would you like someone to be with you?" rather than feel, "Well, I don't know what to say so I think I'll stay away."

Perhaps you've experienced this yourself, if so you know the pain a friend may be experiencing. We call it rejection.

Over the years I've heard so many inappropriate remarks that intensify hurt and grief. I shudder over some of them. And, yes, sometimes I react in anger over comments that I can't believe anyone would make. It could be it's not just a friend but you who have been on the receiving end of such comments over the years. The examples in this chapter are given as a guide of what *not* to say. I wish every church would give these "things not to say" comments to every person in the congregation.

What *Not* to Say When Comforting Someone

- "I don't understand why you're still crying. Life goes on, you know."
- "Look, you only lost your stepfather. What about your mother? She has a greater loss than you, and she's pulled herself together."

- "No one should feel that way about losing a cat. It's only an animal. You had it for ten years. You can find another one."
- "This will make your family closer. It's an opportunity to grow together."
- "I'm sure this will teach the other college students to be more diligent in their studies."
- "Don't you appreciate what you have left?"
- "Next time we'll be sure not to use that doctor or hospital."
- "You've started out in new jobs before, so just look at this layoff as a great opportunity—like George did when he got fired."
- "Be brave."
- "You shouldn't feel that way. After all, you have the Lord."
- "It's time to pull yourself together. You wouldn't want Mother seeing you that way, would you?"
- "The past needs to be put behind us. Let's move on to the future with God."
- "At least he didn't suffer."
- "Well, just be glad it wasn't your only child."
- "Look at it this way. Losing your husband this young and being without children will make it easier for you to handle."
- "Everyone dies sooner or later. He just died sooner."
- "The children need you to be strong."
- "If you'd had a burglar alarm in your home, this never would have happened."
- "This must be God's will."

Statements like these *do not* help or comfort. They only intensify the person's feelings of loss and despair. Along with what *not* to say, churches need to include what *to* say (we'll cover some of these in chapter 9). What a difference this information can make in the lives of people we hope to help!

Sometimes people take an "It could have been worse" approach with their grieving friend in the hope of lessening the hurt. Unfortunately, at this point in time it doesn't work. In *Survival Guidelines for Widows*, Betty Wylie describes this interaction:

> I have one friend who, whenever we got together, at one point would nod her head wisely and say sententiously, "There are worse things than death." It was home-truth time, and she wanted me to know how lucky I was that I didn't have a living vegetable tied up to tubes in the hospital or a human skeleton wasting away with pain in front of my eyes. I know, I know. We are given enough strength, I hope, to bear our own pain. I would not trade with others, nor they with me, in all likelihood...But the widow doesn't feel very lucky and resents being reminded that she still owes a debt of gratitude. She'll come around to it.[9]

In her dramatic and sensitively written book *The Fire That Will Not Die*, Michele McBride gives numerous accounts of the thoughtless, sometimes devastating comments people made that added to her severe physical and psychological pain:

> It was embarrassing for me and my friends when a stranger stopped on the street to ask what happened to my face. This startled all of us, and everyone felt bad—and I never knew exactly what to say. People were crude and said things like, "Are you contagious?" and "Should you be out in public?" Once someone told me I should stay home and not frighten people on the streets. I tried to force myself into believing these people did not mean to be cruel...

> Another time I was in a store with my girlfriend, and we stood paralyzed in horror as a man grabbed the scarf off my head to display my facial scars to another person. The hurt

I was experiencing from those onslaughts was worse than all the pain I endured in the hospital when all the bandages were pulled off my body.[10]

Julie Breuninger, founder of "Face to Face," a support group for parents of children with craniofacial disfigurements, relates some of her experiences in an article in *Today's Christian Woman*. Julie's son, Jonathan, has Crouzon syndrome, a malformation of the skull and face caused by a premature closing of the skull's suture lines. "Our society places so much value on beauty that people just couldn't accept Jonathan. We would go to McDonald's and kids would ask why he looked so funny or parents would look away. When they'd hear him talk, they'd act surprised. They assumed he was retarded."[11]

Why do people react this way? How should they react? Again, the answers come from those who know best: the people who have suffered loss or disfigurement. In a newsletter article published by the Phoenix Society, a national organization providing self-help services to burn survivors and their families, these answers were given by Alan Breslau:

> It is perfectly normal to be alarmed at something or someone who looks out of the ordinary because it or they might present a threat...The disfigured person is going to be cautiously examined to ascertain if there is any threat being presented. The other reason is that no one has taught us how to deal with people who are disfigured. When a child stares and the mother says, "Don't look at him like that!" she is giving the wrong message. Not noticing disfigurement is as bad as staring because if the disfigurement is obvious then by looking away you are sending the message: "discomfort."
>
> As a disfigured person, I feel much more comfortable when people are direct and ask, "What happened to you?" By facing the reality, I can satisfy their curiosity, put them at ease, and probably make a friend. With the mother with the child, I confront her and say, "It's all right for her to look because I do look different, and it is normal to be curious."

Then I tell them both how it happened. Now I have two new friends. [12]

If we had some way of telling everyone how to deal with the disfigured, neither party would then feel uncomfortable. A mother who lost her child shared her painful experience:

> All too common were the reminders. "You can have other babies," as if this baby were replaceable. Don't get pregnant too soon. You don't want to replace this baby." Then they would add, "But be glad you can have others."

> People say things to console themselves. There is no need to try to say things to make you feel better because *there is not a thing they can say—not a word, not a phrase—that will make you feel better about your loss.*

That statement is full of insight and wisdom. You can't take your friend's pain away. You can't fix others. People can't do that. None of us is the Great Healer, Jesus Christ.

Erin Linn compiled and categorized some of the painful and glib clichés thrown about so easily:

"Be Strong" Clichés

Big boys don't cry.
Children are flexible…they will bounce back.
You must be strong for the children.
Support groups are for wimps.
You've just got to get a hold of yourself.
Others have held up well. You can too.
Cheer up.
No sense crying over spilled milk.
This is nature's way.

"Hurry Up" Clichés

You're not your old self.
Out of sight, out of mind.

Time will heal.

You're young, and you will be able to make a new life for yourself.

I just don't understand your behavior.

Life goes on.

No sense dwelling on the past.

"Guilt" Clichés

If you look around, you can always find someone who is worse off than yourself.

This is the work of the devil (which means that if you had a closer relationship with God, the devil could not have had his way).

If I were you, I would do it this way.

Count your blessings.

Only the good die young.

If you had been a better Christian, this would not have happened to you.

Think of all your precious memories.

It's a blessing.

"God" Clichés

God needs him more than you do.

He is happy now because he's with God.

God did this to show how powerful He can be in your life.

It was God's will.

God never gives us more than we can handle.

God helps those who help themselves.

"Discount" Clichés

I know just how you feel.

Silence is golden.

If there is anything I can do, just call me.

You can have more children.

It's better to have loved and lost than never to have loved at all.

Be glad you don't have a problem like mine.
What you don't know won't hurt you.[13]

The Extent of Pain

How would David, who wrote many of the psalms in the Bible, have responded to such comments? The extent of your friend's pain is probably reflected in David's writing:

> Have mercy on me, LORD, for I am faint;
>> heal me, LORD, for my bones are in agony.
> My soul is in deep anguish.
>> How long, LORD, how long?
> Turn, LORD, and deliver me;
>> save me because of your unfailing love.
> Among the dead no one proclaims your name.
>> Who praises you from the grave?
> I am worn out from my groaning.
> All night long I flood my bed with weeping
>> and drench my couch with tears.
> My eyes grow weak with sorrow...
>> (Psalm 6:2-7).

What would you have said to David? How would you have comforted him?

What makes these painful, often-unintended remarks so harmful is that most are from well-intentioned acquaintances. People don't intend to be miserable comforters. A mother once said, "Someone told me it's probably a good thing she did die so she wouldn't suffer. It tore me up for someone to say it was a good thing for a child to die. They haven't been there themselves. Another person said, 'Maybe it's a good thing she died because when she got older, she might have gotten into all kinds of trouble.'" Statements of this nature add to the existing pain.

An all-too-common remark made to parents of children with cancer or a mental handicap is, "You must be a special person. God must really love you to give you a child like this." Is this what a parent feels?

As one mother said, "I'm not special. I don't want to do this either. In essence the person is saying, 'God would never pick me for such things because I'm not strong.' I'm not that strong. And even if I were, I'd rather my child was well or normal."

And then there are the medical "experts," who give parents unsolicited advice about chemotherapy for their children. They'll say, "I wouldn't give her that stuff; people died from that." Parents struggle to make difficult decisions. It's an overwhelming responsibility. But then people who don't know anything about the specifics or what the parents have already gone through question them. Parents in such circumstances would rather hear, "What helped you come to this decision?" or "That must have been a hard decision to make."

One of the best ways I've discovered and recommend to help someone explain her situation and her needs is to write and photocopy a letter she can give to relatives, friends, acquaintances, and anyone else who offers an opinion or asks about what's going on. The letter states what has happened, what it is and will be like for her and her family, what others can expect, and what they can do for the people involved if interested. By doing this, some of the pain is lessened by heading off inappropriate comments and not having to tell the same story over and over. Sometimes the repetition intensifies the pain. Here's an example of a good letter from a family in crisis:

Dear Friend,

You may have heard that we've had some difficulty with our oldest daughter. This has been very hard for my husband and me, and sometimes we're embarrassed over what has happened. Who would have expected that she would use drugs, leave high school, and live on the streets? The reason for this letter is that it's too painful to have to explain this over and over and over to our friends and relatives. We wish the problem would go away or we could just hide. But it doesn't, and we can't, and we don't have any idea how this is going to turn out or when it will be over.

Please just keep asking how we're doing and continue to pray for us. We probably won't be the same each time you talk with us. We could be angry one time and depressed and dejected another time. Help us to talk and just listen. If you have some suggestions, we will consider them, and perhaps something you say will benefit us.

You may find yourself with many questions as well as feelings too. You may be shocked and find yourself angry, wishing you could talk to our daughter and knock some sense into her head. You may even wonder, as we did, where we went wrong. What could we have done differently so this would not have happened? If you hear anyone judging us, please let them know we are already doing this and need their understanding.

Please don't withdraw from us. We need your support more than ever. Pray for us as well as our daughter. We want to continue to love her, encourage her, and believe in her. Pray that we won't just concentrate on our hurt, but also on her needs as well. Don't be surprised if we call you from time to time and say we need to talk, or ask you to go to dinner and talk about anything other than our daughter, since we need a break.

This is a loss to us and to our other children, and it's painful.

Thank you for your support.

When your friend can take a positive, assertive step by reaching out to others to let them know what she needs, she'll gain confidence and strength. She'll feel less like a victim. Above all, she needs to talk about her feelings and concerns with family members. Encourage her not to try to protect them from the news, no matter what the problem, and to be aware of the danger of neglecting them because of all the attention given to the problem person.

Perhaps these words of advice from a hurting person summarize what's best not to do and what to do.

Please

PLEASE, don't ask me if I'm over it yet.
    I'll never be over it.
PLEASE, don't tell me she's in a better place.
    She isn't here with me.
PLEASE, don't say at least she isn't suffering.
    I haven't come to terms with why she had to suffer
    at all.
PLEASE, don't tell me you know how I feel
    unless you've lost a child.
PLEASE, don't ask me if I feel better.
    Bereavement isn't a condition that clears up.
PLEASE, don't tell me at least you had her for so many
    years.
    What year would you choose for your child to die?
PLEASE, don't tell me God never gives us
    more than we can bear.
PLEASE, just say you are sorry.
PLEASE, just say you remember my child, if you do.
PLEASE, just let me talk about my child.
PLEASE, just let me cry.[14]

Chapter 3

If You Want to Help, Listen

If you want to help someone, be there for him. Your presence does wonders. If you want to help someone, listen. One of the greatest gifts one person can give to another is the gift of listening. There is a difference between hearing and listening. Far too many people in conversations only *hear* one another. Few actually listen. One person said that if we could listen to all the conversations in the world, we would discover that, for the most part, they are dialogues of the deaf. Do you know what it's like to really listen to your friend? Not just hear, but really listen? We can draw inspiration from these Scripture verses that reveal how God listens to us:

> The eyes of the LORD are toward the righteous, and His ears are open to their cry. The face of the LORD is against evildoers, to cut off the memory of them from the earth. The righteous cry and the LORD hears, and delivers them out of all their troubles. The LORD is near to the brokenhearted, and saves those who are crushed in spirit (Psalm 34:15-18 NASB).

> I love the LORD, because He hears my voice and my supplications. Because He has inclined His ear to me, therefore I shall call upon Him as long as I live (Psalm 116:1-2 NASB).

> Anyone who answers without listening is foolish and confused (Proverbs 18:13 NCV).

Any story sounds true until someone tells the other side
and sets the record straight (Proverbs 18:17 TLB).

The wise man learns by listening; the simpleton can learn
only by seeing scorners punished (Proverbs 21:11 TLB).

Let every man be quick to hear [a ready listener] (James 1:19
AMP, brackets in original).

Helping people means your ears and your eyes are open to them.
What do I mean by listening? What do I mean by hearing? Is there
really a difference? Definitely. *Hearing* involves gaining content or
information for your own purposes. This *isn't* helping someone. *Listening* involves caring for and being empathetic toward the friend
who is talking. *Hearing* means you're concerned about what's going
on inside you during the conversation. We've all done this. *Listening*
means you're trying to understand the feelings of *the other person* and
are listening for his or her sake. This *is* helping.

What Is Listening Really All About?

Listening means you're not thinking about what you're going to say
when the other person stops talking. You're not busy formulating your
response. Instead, you're concentrating on
what is being said. If a hurting person intrudes
upon your time and space, you're likely to hear
without really listening. Can you stop what
you're doing to give the person your full attention? Yes! It is a choice.

> Real listening
> means you have
> a sincere interest
> in the person's
> feelings and
> opinions.

Listening means that you're completely
accepting of what is being said without judging what your friend is saying or how he is saying it. If you don't like his tone of voice or you
can't condone what he's doing and you react on the spot, you may miss
the meaning of what he's trying to share. Perhaps it isn't being said
in the best way, but listen and accept your friend when he is hurting.

Acceptance doesn't mean that you agree with the content of what he is saying; it simply means you acknowledge and understand that what he's saying is something *he* is feeling right now. This goes such a long way in helping.

Listening means being able to repeat what your friend said and express what you think he is feeling while speaking to you. Real listening means you have a sincere interest in the person's feelings and opinions and are attempting to understand those feelings from his perspective.

Listening to another means letting go of your own concerns, wants, and investments in your own position long enough to consider the friend's concerns, wants, needs, and investment. When you're doing the talking, you're not usually learning. You learn when you listen. And when you listen, it's hard for you to talk.

True listening is a *learnable skill.* Your mind and ears can be taught to hear more keenly; your eyes can be taught to see more clearly. You can also learn to *hear* with your eyes and *see* with your ears. Jesus said, "I speak to them in parables; because while seeing they do not see, and while hearing they do not hear, nor do they understand" (Matthew 13:13 NASB).

The word *hear* in the New Testament doesn't usually refer to an auditory experience. It usually means "to pay heed." As you listen to another person, you need to pay attention to what he is saying *as well as* to what he's not saying or can't say. This requires tuning in to the right frequency. Because my retarded son, Matthew, didn't have a vocabulary, I learned to listen with my eyes. I learned to read the messages in his nonverbal signals. This skill carried over into how I listened to my counselees—hearing what they could put into words and what they couldn't. I learned to listen for the messages behind the message—the hurt, the ache, the frustration, the loss of hope, the fear of rejection, the feeling of betrayal, the joy, the delight, and the promise of change. I also learned to take in what I saw on the person's face and in his posture, walk, and pace. Then I would share with him what I saw. This gave him an opportunity to explain further what he was thinking and feeling. He knew I was tuned in to him.

Your friend needs to sense that you're in sync with him. Listen with your eyes for what he can't put into words. Every message your friend shares has three parts: (1) the actual content, (2) the tone of voice, and (3) the nonverbal communication. It's possible to use the same word, statement, or question and express many different messages simply by changing tone of voice or body movement. Nonverbal communication includes facial expressions, body postures, and gestures or actions.

It's been suggested that successful communication consists of 7 percent content, 38 percent tone of voice, and 55 percent nonverbal communication.[1] We're usually aware of the content of what we're saying, but not nearly as aware of our tone of voice. We have the capability of giving one sentence a dozen different meanings just by changing our tone. Record some of your conversations and then listen to them. You'll probably be amazed. When you say with a serious, I'm interested tone of voice, "I want to hear what you have to say," but then bury your head in paperwork or check your watch, what will your friend believe? When you ask, "How was your day?" in a flat tone while walking beside him, what will he probably respond to—the verbal or nonverbal message? That's right. The nonverbal cues usually override the verbal cues. Sometimes you may wonder why your friend responded in a different way than you expected. It could have been your tone, your nonverbal cues, or the fact that he was emotionally upset so his perceptions were impaired.

Types of Listening

Some people listen for facts, information, and details for their own use. Others listen because they feel sorry for the person. Some who listen are nothing more than voyeurs who have an incessant need to pry and probe into people's lives. Your friend doesn't need this. On occasion, people listen out of obligation, out of necessity, or to be polite. If you do, your friend will pick up on it. Some people listen because they care. Sensitive listening and hearing are like

> Sensitive listening and hearing are like mine shafts to the heart.

mine shafts to the heart when ministering to others. But all too often the potential for listening lies buried within us like hidden gold because of barriers that inhibit our listening capacity.

Why do you listen? What are your motives? Listening that springs from caring builds closeness, reflects love, and is an act of grace. This is the type of listening Jesus calls us to do. When you paraphrase what your friend is saying back to him, he knows you're interested and listening so he'll continue to talk. And when you verbally accept what he says (which isn't necessarily agreeing with what he says), he will likely share even more.

Overcoming Listening Obstacles

Why do people listen to others? Partly because we've been taught to do so, but there are four basic reasons why we listen to other people:

- to understand someone (a hurting person needs this)
- to enjoy the other person (even though you may not enjoy him at this time)
- to learn something from the one talking (you will, and it may shock you)
- to give help, assistance, or comfort to the person (this is a major reason)

The world is made up of many pseudo-listeners who masquerade as real friends. But anyone who doesn't listen for those four reasons most likely only hears what others are saying. For *caring listening* to occur and continue, we need to be aware of some of the common obstacles that can interrupt that ability so we can guard against them.

Defensiveness

You will miss part if not all the message if your mind is busy thinking up a rebuttal, excuse, or exception to what your friend is saying. There is a variety of defensive responses. Perhaps you reach a *premature conclusion*. "All right. I know just what you're going to say." *Impatience hits.* Some who are in a crisis give you one sentence, go silent for a minute, and then utter another sentence, and then comes more silence. It could take her several minutes to complete her thought. Don't get impatient. Wait and honor your friend's pauses. The delays could be because of her state of mind or she could be an introvert. Introverts often need time to think before they speak, and they typically take around seven seconds before they answer a question.

Rehearsing your response (as well as other defensive postures) is not what the Scriptures call us to do as caring listeners. Remember this verse from earlier? "Anyone who answers without listening is foolish and confused" (Proverbs 18:13 NCV). When you're formulating what you're going to say or do, you've detached from listening or even quit listening.

> Give the hurting person the opportunity to disagree...Your goal isn't to convince her of something you believe.

Explosive or inflammatory words from your friend create an inner eruption of emotions within you. Not only will you react to your friend's words, but you also may consciously or subconsciously choose to respond in kind, using words that you know will incite your friend, making it difficult for the other person to listen well.

Hurting people are highly sensitive. Expect to hear thoughts, words, and phrases you don't like, don't accept, or don't agree with when you're reaching out to a hurting person. If you have difficulty hearing anger, resentment, or bitterness, watch out because that's probably what's coming. Let the person share with you. Don't make judgments, offer corrections, or share your view. Just listen.

Not all defensiveness is overtly expressed. Outwardly you might be agreeing, but inside you're saying just the opposite. The hurting person could be doing this too. Give her the opportunity to disagree with whatever you share. Your goal isn't to convince her of something you believe.

Bias

You may have a biased attitude toward a person who speaks in a certain tone of voice, is a member of a certain ethnic group, is of the opposite sex, reminds you of a person from your past, and so forth. We all struggle with bias to some degree. Bias might cause you to reject a person or a personality without really listening to what the person has to say. In effect you're saying, "I don't like people who are [*character-istic*]. If you do this [*behavior*], I don't need to listen to you." You will encounter this. Expect it and plan for it. Know that you can't hide it. Most of the time your body language will give you away. You may experience this when an acquaintance comes for help, or you may be shocked at seeing a side of your friend you've never seen.

Personal bias affects how well you listen. It may be easier for you to listen to an angry person than to a sarcastic person. You may find some voice intonations more enjoyable to listen to, while others may be annoying. The repetitive phrases a person uses (and might not be aware of) could bother you. (You can expect repetition when someone is upset or devastated.) Excessive gestures, such as talking with the hands or waving the arms, can be overly distracting and uncomfortable for you. Perhaps you're distracted from listening because of the speaker's gender. You're influenced by your expectations of what is appropriate for a man or a woman to share or not share.

Have any of these distractions happened to you? The stereotypes you assign to people influence how you listen to them. We all would like to believe we're free from negative bias, but no one is.

Listening Styles

Some people hear with optimism; others hear with pessimism. I might hear bad news, and you might hear good news. If your friend shares a frustrating and difficult situation, you may stop listening because you see her situation as petty or insignificant. Or you may listen more closely because you view her sharing as an act of trust in you. On which side of the coin do you live? Generally optimistic or generally pessimistic?

Lack of understanding gender differences in listening and conversation creates problems. Women tend to use more verbal responses to encourage the talker. They're more likely than men to use sounds or words to indicate they're listening. Men typically use sounds or words only when they're agreeing with what the person is saying. Can you see what the outcome could be? A man interprets a woman's listening responses as signs that she agrees with him, but later on he discovers she wasn't agreeing with him at all. He didn't realize she was simply indicating her interest in what he was saying to keep the interchange going. A woman, on the other hand, may feel ignored and disappointed because a man doesn't make the same listening responses she does. She notes the lack of verbal cues and interprets the quietness as not listening or disinterest.

Emotional Involvement

People have difficulty listening when their emotional involvement reaches the point where they're unable to separate themselves from the person reaching out for help. This can be a struggle for anyone attempting to help another person. You empathize too much and take the person's burdens on yourself.

For instance, what a friend says may cause threatening feelings to surface in you or it may reactivate your own past hurts. This can hinder your listening capability. Can you think of a time when you listened to another person and felt so overwhelmed with feelings that you were unable to hear what the person was saying? What did you do? How were you able to keep helping your friend?

You may experience difficulty in listening because the person has expectations of you that you're afraid you can't meet…or you don't want to meet.

Then there are the physical components. If someone speaks too loudly or too softly, you may struggle to keep listening.

Responding to Distractions

All of these listening distractions can and will happen when you reach out to help others or when they reach out to you for help. Being aware of them and their potential is a good place to start. How do you deal with distractions? Here are some suggestions for countering distractions and keeping focused.

Interrupting

When you feel like the other person isn't getting to the point fast enough, you may start asking for information that would be forthcoming eventually. Have you found yourself saying, "Hold it! I've got a dozen ideas cooking because of what you said. Let me tell you some of my suggestions"? It's easy for your mind to wander because people think at five times the rate they speak. If a person speaks at 100 words a minute and you're listening at the rate of 500 words per minute, what do you do during the gap? Even though you process information faster than it can be verbalized, you *choose* to stay in pace with the speaker or you *choose* to let your mind wander. If you're extroverted in personality, you'll struggle with listening when the information is slow in coming. Extroverts have to work at not interrupting or jumping in when there are silences in the conversation.

Mental Overload

The person you're helping may overload you with information. You feel bombarded with all the details and don't have enough time to digest them. Your mind feels like a juggler with too many items. This makes it difficult to listen to anything. I suggest you relax and catch the basic themes of what is going on. You can go over the details later if you feel the need.

Bad Timing

What if the person wants to talk when you don't? Have you made comments such as, "Talk now? Well, this isn't the best time," or "Just a minute—I need to finish this first," or "I'd like to listen, but I'm already late for an appointment"? Choosing the right time to listen can be crucial to the communication process. Hurting people often approach others at bad times or with little warning. If you can shift gears and adapt into listening mode, great. If you can't, set up a later time to meet with your friend.

Physical Exhaustion

Mental and physical fatigue make it difficult to listen. There are times when you need to let your friend know that right now isn't a good time. Be sure to let him know that you do want to hear what he has to say and set up a time to talk when you'll be refreshed and alert.

Selective Attention

Another name for this obstacle is "filtered listening." It's when you screen the information being shared. If you tend to be pessimistic, you may ignore, distort, or reject positive messages. Often people hear what they want to hear or what fits within their mindset. When you engage in selective listening, you probably are also engaging in selective retention. That means you'll remember only some of the comments and situations mentioned.

To combat this obstacle, regularly reflect back to the person what you're hearing. Take deep breaths occasionally to stay alert. Ask yourself, "I'm listening carefully, but what am I not hearing?"

Do you know what hinders you from listening?

Listen with Your Entire Body

To help you stay focused, concentrate on the person and the message. Give your friend your undivided attention. Turn off the TV when your friend calls to talk. Set aside what you're doing and listen carefully. When you listen with your heart, you're helping. A pastor friend told me of being called to the home of a man who had just lost his wife. When he came into the house, the man wept and hugged him. The husband sat down. The pastor sat down on the couch next to him and decided to wait and allow the husband to take the lead in saying something. He waited for an hour listening to the sounds of silence. He waited for a second hour, still listening to the quiet. The bereaved man sighed. My friend broke the silence. "Are you hungry? Would you like me to get us a pizza?"

He said, "Oh, yes, that would be great." So the pastor did. He brought it back, and they ate. They each said a few words. My friend prayed briefly, patted the grieving husband on the shoulder, and left. Several weeks later he was surprised to hear that this man had told a number of people he'd been helped by the pastor coming over and just spending time with him. Could you have done that? Of course! Your time and presence may be all your friend needs right now. Be present. Harold Kushner describes this type of ministering in his book *Living a Life that Matters*:

> At some of the darkest moments of my life, some people I thought of as friends deserted me—some because they cared about me and it hurt them to see me in pain; others because I reminded them of their own vulnerability, and that was more than they could handle. But real friends overcame their discomfort and came to sit with me. If they had no words to make me feel better they sat in silence (much better than saying "You'll get over it," or "It's not so bad; others have it worse"), and I loved them for it.[2]

Remember...

> The bereaved need to be listened to, not supplied with answers. They know deep down that there are no explanations to most important questions they are asking themselves, and they aren't really expecting answers from those who console them. Mourning has to be lived through; it cannot be resolved with intellectual responses. Being an accepting and caring presence and a good listener is one of the greatest gifts one person can give to another in grief.[3]

Remember...

> Something happens when we listen
>   not just with our ears
>   but with our eyes.
> Something happens when we wait out
>   a griever's words.

Something happens when we express our care
    in calming ways.
Something happens when we keep our promises
    even when less than convenient.
Something happens when we pay attention
    to the questions of the griever
    rather than offer a cheap answer.
Something happens when hearts touch.
Something happens when we remember Jesus' promise
    "Where two or three are gathered…
    there I will be, too."
Something happens when a caregiver
    Becomes a grief sharer. [4]

Harold Ivan Smith

I've found this prayer helps me be the listener God wants me to be:

O, God, a great deal of our life is spent listening to others.
Help us always to listen in the right way.
    Help us to listen with attention, not to let our
    thoughts wander, to concentrate on what we hear,
    that it may really stay in our minds, and not go into
    one ear and out the other.
Help us to listen and to understand,
    Help us not to give up thinking, questioning, enquir-
    ing, until we really find what a thing means.
Help us to listen and to remember.
    Help us not to hear, and then go away and forget all
    about what we have heard. Give us minds which are
    interested, for only then can we have memories which
    are retentive.
Help us to listen and to act.
    Help us to put into practice that which we are taught,
    both at our day's work and at our instruction in the

faith. Help us to remember always that words are poor things without deeds, and that faith without works is dead.

And so grant that hearing, understanding, remembering and doing may ever go hand in hand.[5]

Chapter 4

Understanding What Your Friend
Is Experiencing

Life is full of losses. In fact, life is a blending of loss and gain, loss and acquisition. Any event that destroys our understanding of the meaning of life is felt as a loss. We feel our beliefs and expectations are under attack. Losses can be obvious—a stolen car, a burglarized house, or losing a loved one through death or divorce. Other losses may not be so obvious. Changing jobs, receiving a B instead of an A in a study course, receiving a less-than-hoped-for amount in a raise, moving, illness (loss of health), a new teacher mid-semester, the change from an office with windows to one without, success and achievement (the loss of striving, or challenge, or even relationships with fellow workers), and a son or daughter going off to school. The disappearance of an ideal, a dream, or a lifelong goal are losses also. Because these losses may not be easy to recognize, we don't typically identify them as such. As one person said, "There's no casserole parade for those losses." Therefore, most don't spend time and energy dealing with them.

Many of the losses in life are related to aging. As we grow older the dreams and beliefs of childhood crumble and change.

The job market contains many losses. Someone else gets the raise or promotion, deals fall through, court cases are lost, businesses fail, the economy falters, we get stuck in a "going nowhere" job.

Then we see the physical losses—a major one involves the gain of pounds and inches. We lose our youth, beauty, smooth skin, muscle tone, shape, hair, vision, hearing, and diminishing sexual ability and interest.

The loss of children (when they move out and establish their own families) can be complicated. For some it also involves the loss of identity as a parent, the loss of influence over the children, the loss of dreams or feelings of success if the children didn't turn out well, and the loss of marriage if the children were the glue that kept the parents together.

Losing a spouse when someone is older is limiting as well, but for women it is even more difficult. Most women over the age of fifty who lose their husbands do not remarry. If a person divorces or a spouse dies when his or her mate is still young, it is much easier to find another mate.[1]

When the word *loss* is mentioned, death and divorce come to mind. But what about the impact of a negative medical diagnosis? "The doctor said it was cancer [or multiple sclerosis or Parkinson's or Alzheimer's]." Or perhaps an accident causes a permanent loss of function. That is a state of chronic grief. Where is the ritual in our culture to commemorate the grief of a lifelong disability?

Some of the hardest losses to deal with are the ones that "threaten." The *possibility* of losing something is always present, and there is little that we can do about them. Our sense of control is destroyed. We've worked for so many years at a company. At twenty years all of our benefits will be secure. But then we're informed that due to the sluggish economy and lost contracts, 40 percent of the firm's employees will be terminated at the end of the month—and length of employment is not a criterion for being retained. Will we be one of the 40 percent? There are many other threatened losses in life, including:

- awaiting the outcome of a biopsy
- a spouse saying, "I'm thinking of divorcing you"
- a business investment that may not come through
- being sued by an angry employee or customer

- being in a foreign country when the government threatens to detain everyone as hostages

- a friend saying he suspects your son has been using drugs

These potential losses could occur, and we feel them as losses when we worry or anticipate them. We feel helpless.

Types of Losses

The losses people experience can be grouped in numerous ways. One is *material loss*. This is the loss of a physical object or even familiar surroundings to which a person has an important attachment.

A *relationship loss* is the ending of opportunities to relate to another person. No longer being able to talk, share experiences, touch, negotiate, debate, or be in the emotional and physical presence of a friend. This loss can come from a move, a divorce, a death, the process of growing up, or conflict.

Intrapsychic losses are when your friend's perceptions or the way he views himself undergoes a change. He loses an emotionally important image of himself as well as the possibilities of what might have been.

There is *functional loss*, such as the muscular or neurological function of the physical body going haywire. This comes with age, but it also can occur throughout life from various causes. *Memory loss* among the elderly can be devastating.

Role loss impacts all of us. It's when a person experiences the loss of a social role or accustomed place in a social network. The significance depends on how much of his identity was tied to a particular role. A promotion, demotion, loss of spouse, change of career, graduating or dropping out of school, or retirement fit here.

While experiencing loss, questions fester beneath the surface. At some point they need to be addressed. If your friend has suffered a loss, you may hear comments like these:

- "Will I recover from this loss? Will I survive?"

- "Is it all right to continue with my life without [whatever or whomever]?"

- "Can I be happy and fulfilled knowing that the person I've lost is really gone and my life will now be different?"

The Loss of a Family Member

The loss of significant people in our lives is inevitable. Often this type of loss happens suddenly and traumatically, but at other times the loss is expected. Either way, this can be a tremendous crisis and may bring a significant loss of identity for your friend. (If you know the person whom your friend has lost, you'll be feeling a loss as well. To help your friend, some of the intensity of your own grief may have to be put on hold for a while.) Everyone experiences loss, and eventually everyone has to deal with death. For example, in the last twenty-six years I've lost four cousins, two uncles, a sister-in-law, my mother, my mother-in-law, my son, my wife, the son of one of my closest friends, and two of my beloved golden retrievers.

When the loss is a highly significant person in your friend's life, he will feel pain. Nothing and no one can prepare anyone for the extent of that pain. Has anyone told your friend, or you for that matter, what to expect when there is a loss of a parent, sibling, child, or friend? I doubt it because it's not something we talk about much even though everyone experiences it at some point and grieves when a major loss like this occurs. Counselors call this process "grief work" because *grieving is work.*

When your friend lost a significant person, he started grieving over the person he lost, but he also grieves over losing the wishes, needs, hopes, dreams, and expectations he had for the person and the relationship. These are important aspects of grief you can help your friend identify. He is grieving not just for his present loss, but for what he lost from the future. Perhaps there was something he never had in his relationship with that person, and now he realizes he'll never have it. Over the years I've worked with numerous women who didn't have good relationships with their fathers. When the fathers died, that shut the door on any hope the daughters had for reconciliation.

When your friend loses a significant person in a sudden, unexpected death, he's at high risk for a pattern of complicated grieving.

This includes those who lost loved ones in terrorist attacks, such as the one on September 11, 2001, public shootings, such as the ones at Fort Hood in Texas, and traumas, such as automobile accidents and plane crashes. The survivors of those situations also deal with grief. Sometimes that type of grief evolves into a condition known as Post Traumatic Stress Disorder (PTSD).

Why does grief seem to escalate at times? Consider the cumulative effect of the following factors shared by Therese Rando in her book *Grieving: How to Go On Living When Someone You Love Dies*:

- Your assumptions about control, predictability, and security are lost.

- Your loss makes no sense whatever.

- It's difficult to recognize the loss.

- You can't even say goodbye or conclude any unfinished business.

- Your emotional reactions are heightened much more than when a natural death occurs.

- Your symptoms of grief and shock persist, which demoralizes you.

- You may tend to hold yourself responsible more than you normally would.

- You experience a profound loss of security and confidence in your world. In fact, you're shattered.

- You tend to focus on the negative aspects of the relationship with the deceased, rather than having a balanced view.

- You have sudden major secondary losses because of the unexpectedness of the loss.[2]

You may be thinking, *I could never help a friend dealing with that many issues in this type of situation.* But you can. The more you know and understand grief, the more you can help. In many cases you may be the only support someone has at the moment.

As your friend recovers from a significant crisis or loss, at times he may be *ambushed* by grief (and it could hit you as well). There is no better way to describe it, although some call it a "grief spasm." It's a sudden onslaught of grief that hits a person when he least expects it. He may choke up or cry, his chest may feel constricted, and a wave of sadness may overwhelm him. This attack is normal even though it doesn't feel like it. When it occurs, advise your friend that he needs to stop everything else and deal with his feelings or they will persist and, perhaps, intensify.[3]

The purpose of helping your friend face his grief is to help him come to the place where he can accept and live with the loss of a significant person in a healthy way. You'll probably be asked, "How long will this take?" But you can't give a precise answer because there are many factors to consider. There are, however, some general patterns you can share with your friend as an encouragement.

One of the tasks during grief is to learn how to function without the significant person. Your friend won't have the interactions and validations he experienced with that person. Talking about this aspect of loss may be helpful for him. The loss of the physical presence in his life means that his needs, hopes, dreams, expectations, feelings, and thoughts will change. Slowly the reality of separation will sink in, and he'll realize, "For now I exist without this person as part of my life. I can do this." This is an important place to arrive.

Your friend may discover that it will take time to identify all the ways the significant individual impacted his life. It's a step-by-step process. The loss of companionship, support, judgment, advice—all of these new and separate losses make up the major loss.

Each time he starts to respond to the person who is no longer there, he'll discover again that he is gone and feel the pain. And there will be many painful reminders. Your friend may say to you, "I turned to him to take care of a task he usually handled for me. Then I realized again that he's gone."

Whenever someone is gone from a person's life, the survivor's roles and skills have to broaden to function without the other person. Your friend will need to learn how to make up for what he's lost. He'll have to change some of what he does, take on new responsibilities, and, perhaps, find other people to relate to and help. There may be some things he won't do anymore. Adjustment necessitates not behaving the same way he did when the person was a part of his world. (This is also true when anyone loses a significant activity through job loss, expulsion from school, house foreclosure, and so forth.)

When the person you're helping has experienced a loss, he's plunged into grief. Most people in our culture have never been taught the grieving process, so they end up thinking that something is wrong with them, that they're going crazy. Grief takes on *many* faces in someone's life, including disruptions, holes, and confusion. It disrupts a person's schedule too. And the ensuing grief doesn't just impact one part of the person. No, it comes from within and doesn't leave one particle of life untouched. It's all-consuming. There are body changes. Food doesn't taste the same, nor will the fragrance of a favorite flower be as intense. Frequent tears will cloud his vision often and at unexpected moments. Some people experience a tightness in their stomach, shortness of breath, and/or rapid heartbeat. Eating and sleeping patterns won't be the same. Some people sleep and sleep, while others wish that sleep would come. Sleep will be either an easy escape or elusive. Weird dreams or nightmares occur. These disruptions will decrease in time, but recovery isn't a smooth, straightforward path. It's more like a forward–backward dance.

If grief occurs because of the death of a loved one, the survivor's life has now been divided into two segments—life before the death and life after the death. This change can bring out the best in a person as well as the worst. When dealing with grief many people struggle and ask, "What is wrong with me?" Their thoughts trail off, their concentration is nonexistent, and memory deficits become the norm.

Prior to the death of a loved one, life was going in a well-established direction. This has changed. Before the death, there was a firm identity. The people involved could say who they were. This too has changed. They aren't exactly who they were. The person who died was part of their identity. He was someone's father, uncle, spouse, brother, and friend. The person will continue to be that person in their hearts and memories, but there's a vacant physical place where the loved one stood. The loss of this person has subtracted part of who they were. Eventually they will take steps to move from the old to the new identity.[4] This may be hard for them to grasp now, but someday they will.

Some people may also experience "face in the crowd" syndrome. They think they've seen the one they lost, or heard his voice, or smelled his cologne. This can happen at home and in public places. The people may wake up at night and swear they sensed the deceased person's presence in the room or heard the person call their names. They think they're going crazy so hesitate to share their experience with others for fear of what they will think. But this phenomena is more common than most realize, and it can last for as long as eighteen months.

How can you help? One thing you can do is make a copy of the following "Crazy Feelings of Grief" list and share it with your friend. This will help him realize what he's going through is normal. Many people believe they're odd or going crazy, and reading this list can "normalize" what they're experiencing. When I ask people who have read the list which ones they've experienced, many look at me and say, "All of the above!"

Another option is to give them a copy of my book *Experiencing Grief*. It will help them understand what they're going through. (If you're regularly ministering to those in grief, you'll find it helpful to read *Grieving the Loss of a Family Member*, *Helping Those in Grief*, and *When a Child Is Missing*.)

The "crazy" feelings of grief are actually *sane* responses to loss. The following examples are all symptoms of *normal* grief:

Crazy Feelings of Grief

- distorted thinking patterns, "crazy" and/or irrational thoughts, fearful thoughts
- feelings of despair and hopelessness
- out of control or numbed emotions

- changes in sensory perceptions (sight, taste, smell, touch, hearing)
- increased irritability
- may want to talk a lot or not at all
- memory lags and mental short-circuits
- inability to concentrate
- obsessive focus on the lost loved one
- losing track of time
- increase or decrease of appetite and/or sexual desire
- difficulty falling or staying asleep
- dreams in which the deceased seems to visit
- nightmares with repeated death themes
- physical illnesses like the flu, headaches, or other maladies
- shattered beliefs about life, the world, and even God

Grieving takes longer than most people imagine. It tends to intensify at three months, on special dates, and on the one-year anniversary of the loss.[5]

Since many have difficulty going to or staying asleep, it might be helpful to suggest that your friend read the following Scriptures and say the prayer by Michael Leunig out loud each night prior to turning off the light. Many people have found this beneficial.

> When you lie down, you shall not be afraid; yes, you shall lie down, and your sleep shall be sweet. Be not afraid of sudden terror and panic, nor of the stormy blast or the storm and ruin of the wicked when it comes [for you will be guiltless], for the Lord shall be your confidence, firm and strong, and shall keep your foot from being caught [in a trap or some hidden danger] (Proverbs 3:24-26 AMP, brackets in original).

I lay down and slept in peace and woke up safely, for the Lord was watching over me (Psalm 3:6 TLB).

If I'm sleepless at midnight, I spend the hours in grateful reflection (Psalm 63:6 MSG).

When my anxious thoughts multiply within me, Your consolations delight my soul (Psalm 94:19 NASB).

In peace I will lie down and sleep, for you alone, LORD, make me dwell in safety (Psalm 4:8).

In a dream, a vision of the night, when sound sleep falls on men, while they slumber in their beds, then He opens the ears of men, and seals their instruction (Job 33:15-16 NASB).

Dear God,

We give thanks for the darkness of the night where lies the world of dreams. Guide us closer to our dreams so that we may be nourished by them. Give us strong dreams and memory of them so that we may carry their poetry and mystery into our daily lives.

Grant us deep and restful sleep that we may wake refreshed with strength enough to renew a world grown tired.

We give thanks for the inspiration of stars, the dignity of the moon, and the lullabies of crickets and frogs.

Let us restore the night and reclaim it as a sanctuary of peace, where silence shall be music to our hearts and darkness shall throw light upon our souls. Good night. Sweet dreams. Amen.[6]

Steps in the Grief Work Process

Getting on with life after a significant loss involves several steps, some of which may come as a surprise to your friend and you if neither of you have been through this before. Few people are aware of these steps before they experience a major loss. Some individuals resist the steps or become stuck in their grief work. Your presence can help keep this from happening to your friend. Sometimes after people have gone through these stages, they're able to sit down and identify what they've experienced. But what a difference it can make in your friend's life if she's aware of the process at the time she's going through it! The awareness won't necessarily lessen the pain, but it gives her a map and lets her know she's on track and not going crazy. These steps apply to the more serious kinds of losses.

One of the first things your friend must do is *develop a new relationship with the person she lost.* She has to untie the ties that connected her to this person. The change involves your friend keeping her loved one alive through memories in a healthy and appropriate manner. Are you comfortable talking with her about this? Is this something you've been through? If she doesn't think about it, you may need to suggest it. (You may want to also suggest she read my book *Recovering from the Losses of Life* or, if her loss was a spouse, *Reflections of a Grieving Spouse.*)

Formation of a new identity without the other person's presence is another step your friend needs to take in her recovery. As one person said, "That portion of my life is history. I'll never be that way or be that person again."

The Loss of a Spouse

Most couples who marry dream of growing old together, so when a death occurs there is not only the loss of that dream but also all sorts of secondary losses. Hopes, wishes, fantasies, feelings, expectations, and the needs that she had for the spouse are gone. There is another loss in her future as well with the death of a spouse. Her identity is now being a widow—single rather than married. That's a bit of an adjustment. When a spouse loses a mate, she loses someone with whom she would have shared retirement, birthdays, the bed, church functions, children and grandchildren, and weddings. Look at all the roles a spouse fulfills and what is lost when that person dies.

bill payer	checkbook balancer	confidant
business partner	companion	cook

counselor	identity prover	prayer partner
couple's class	laundry person	protector
couple's friends	lover	provider
encourager	mechanic	source of inspira-
errand person	mentor	tion and insights
friend	motivator	sports partner
gardener	organizer	tax preparer
handyperson	parent	teacher

As your friend walks through these steps and does her grief work, the emotional energy she once invested in her spouse is now freed up to be reinvested in other people, activities, and hopes that, in turn, bring emotional satisfaction.

Death ends a loved one's life, but it doesn't end your friend's relationship with that person. How does she develop a new relationship with the person she's lost? This isn't a morbid or odd process; it's a normal and necessary response. Yet have you ever heard a discussion about such a change in a relationship? Probably not. If people tell your friend that the best way to deal with her loss is to forget the person, very frankly they're wrong. Your friend won't forget. Someday, way in the future, the emotional memories will become historical memories.

People keep other people alive all the time as they reflect on who the loved ones were, their achievements, and their impacts on people and society. I'm sure you've heard people say, "I wonder what he would think if he were alive today" or "Wouldn't she be surprised to see all of this"? I know I have.

It may help your friend to be with others who have experienced the same type of loss because they can assist her in the process of adjusting to her new identity. You may be one of those people.

The Length of Mourning

How long does it take to complete the mourning process? Much longer than most people believe. The amount of time varies and depends on many factors. The average length of mourning is approximately two years for a natural death. In the case of a terminally ill individual, the time following the death could be less because some of the grieving happened prior to the person's death.

The unanticipated nature of accidental death can be a major factor in contributing to a grief reaction that lasts for several years. One study indicated that the majority of mourners who experienced the loss of a spouse or child in an automobile accident were still dealing with the death in thoughts, memories, and feelings four to seven years afterward.[7] It could take longer if your friend was involved in the same accident. And if the death is the result of trauma, there's no way to predict how long the mourning will last. For many who have lost a child, it can take six to ten years to stabilize.

You can't tell your friend how long his grief will last, but be sure he'll ask because it may seem to him that it's lasting forever. You see, grief does have a beginning, a middle, and an end. But many people get stuck in the middle, and most don't understand the dynamics and the duration of grief. This makes it even more difficult to adjust.

The emotional upheaval associated with bereavement includes a number of common elements: a sense of yearning and searching; sensitivity to stimuli; feelings of anger, guilt, ambiguity, impatience, and restlessness; and a strong need to test what is real. As you can see from the following Phases of Bereavement chart, these feelings intensify and fade.[8]

Phases of Bereavement Intensity

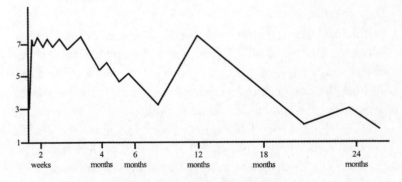

Phases of Bereavement Intensity

Notice the jagged peaks. Pain and grief actually intensify at three months and then gradually subside, but instead of gradually declining, they go up and down. Most people experience a rush of grief and pain at the first-year anniversary of the loss of a loved one that rivals the initial feelings. If anyone tries to tell your friend she should be "over it by now" or "feeling better" at any of those peak times, she may become quite upset, which is understandable. It's also understandable that most people don't appreciate the grief process unless they've been through it themselves.[9]

Time after time I've shown this bereavement chart in seminars, and people have come up and said, "Why didn't someone warn me about the three-month and one-year anniversaries? It would have made it easier to handle. I thought I was going crazy!" Another problem is that most feel that after three months of grieving, a person ought to be doing all right. So they pull away their extra support at a time when the one in grief needs it more than ever.

As I've mentioned, there's another phenomenon your friend may experience but not want to share with you or anyone else: the "face in the crowd" syndrome. She's walking along and would swear she saw her loved one at a gathering or heard her loved one's voice. Or she walked into a room on their anniversary and smelled his cologne. This may seem odd, but it is normal. The grieving person thinks she's weird, abnormal, or going crazy. She's not. These types of experiences can last up to eighteen months after the loss.

The Loss of a Parent

Parental loss we all expect, but that doesn't lessen the impact when it happens. The first death I experienced with a family member came when I was twenty-two. My father was killed in a traffic accident driving home from work. He was seventy-two. What I remember was the devastating news and shock. When my mother died in 1993 at the age of ninety-three, it was a loss but not a shock. Her illness was gradual, and she'd wanted to go to heaven and be with the Lord for several years.

When Dad died, there was a sense of missing out on future events, especially since my wife and I had discovered the week of the accident that we were going to be parents. Losing the first parent can often be a lingering pain because we constantly witness the effects of this loss on the remaining parent. And we may feel added pressure because we feel responsible in a new way for helping this parent.

When someone loses a parent, she loses a person who for many years has been the most influential person in her life. For most of us, losing a parent means losing someone who loved us and cared for us in a way no one else does or ever will. We can no longer gain that parent's approval, praise, or permission. Feelings of attachment to a parent are unique, and now that link to one of them has severed.

When one of her parents dies, your friend loses a direct link to the past as well as to parts of herself she may have forgotten. Not only that, but she will be much more aware of her own mortality. You'll hear your friend express this. What she doesn't need to hear is, "What are you talking about? You're nowhere near that parent's age. That's ridiculous." People feel more vulnerable when one or both of their parents aren't around to help buffer life's ups and downs. When the second parent dies, it's like the last chapter of a book is over. For some it means they can never go home again psychologically or physically. When your friend has to close up her parents' home and sort through what is left, she experiences an abundance of secondary losses.

As we grow older, we often become attached to our parents in a new way. Now it's more of an adult-to-adult or friend-to-friend relationship. I saw this in the closeness of my late wife, Joyce, and her mother. The roles eventually reverse from the parent caring for the child to the child caring for the parent. When Joyce's mother died in her nineties, and even though she wanted the Lord to take her, it was painful for Joyce.

Responses to the death of a parent vary from person to person, depending on the quality of the relationship. One of your friends may grieve extensively and another move right on. If there's been a good relationship with the parent, there's the wish it could continue. There's a feeling of being let down when a parent has been taken away. For others, the loss is also the loss of opportunity to make up for difficulties in the past. Some feel cheated that they lost out on doing more for their parent(s). And for some there may be a sense of relief. They lived with the fear they would someday lose their parents, and now it's a reality. They feel like they can get on with their lives.

For many people, the one they were closest to wasn't a birth parent. It may have been an aunt or uncle or even a surrogate parent. It's important that they face what they're feeling with this loss, experience the fullness of the grief and the secondary losses, and then move forward without the person.

Not all people have good relationships with their parents. This can complicate the grief response. In some cases I've seen a person express relief over the death of a parent. Finally your friend feels freedom from conflict and pain. For some people, it's a new phase of life when they don't have to try to please someone they never could anyway. She may feel relief from the demands she's struggled with for years. Or she may feel relief because her parent's lingering, terminal illness made it difficult to care for him and was financially draining. This may not have been your experience so it might shock you, especially if you hear some very negative comments.

As your friend grieves the loss of a parent, keep in mind her other family members will grieve differently because of the quality of their relationships with the parent. Her siblings, spouse, and children had a different relationship than she did. This could generate conflict between them unless everyone allows for these differences.

When parents are gone, who takes their place or continues their roles? Perhaps they were the peacekeepers for all their children and grandchildren. Who does that now? Perhaps they orchestrated family get-togethers. Who takes on that role now? Decisions concerning home and property must be made and family heirlooms divided up. The passing of parents definitely affects relationships between siblings.[10]

Consideration of some of these changes in advance makes it easier for the surviving family members. These are issues and topics to address at the appropriate time. You might suggest these books to the person you're helping:

H. Norman Wright, *Experiencing Grief.*

H. Norman Wright, *Grieving the Loss of a Family Member.* Chapters include:

- The Loss of a Spouse
- The Death of a Child
- Helping Children in Grief
- The Death of a Parent
- The Loss of a Sibling
- The Loss of a Friend
- The Loss of a Pet

H. Norman Wright, *Missing the Child You Love*

Helping the Terminally Ill

What if a friend discovers she's terminally ill and comes to talk with you about it? Most people find it hard to know what to say to a person who's received such a severe diagnosis. Often they say nothing, which makes them appear uncaring. If you've heard your friend has a serious or terminal illness, open the conversation by saying, "I understand you've been ill lately." *Then take your cues for how to proceed from the person.* If she wants to talk about it, she will. Tune in to her feelings and respond not just to what is said, but also to her nonverbal communication as well. If she chooses not to discuss her illness, allow her that choice. You've acknowledged her illness, given her an opportunity to share, and let her know you care.

The ill person often believes friends will think less of them or not want to do things with them because they're ill. The person thinks she's a less-than-desirable friend now. And some people do have difficulty knowing what to say. Is that an uncommon response? No. Not knowing what to say is probably the most common and frustrating feeling we experience when a friend or loved one is going through a major loss or experience. Everyone struggles with what to say, how to say it, and when to say it. A person's severe illness also makes us think about our own mortality.

Acknowledging that the loss has occurred in this person's life is important. Look at the situation through her eyes rather than your own. Here are some basic introductory questions you can use to show you care:

> "Would you like to tell me what happened? I'd like to hear about it."
>
> "What is each day like for you now?"
>
> "What's your greatest concern at this time?"
>
> "Tell me about your sleeping and eating these days."

Chapter 5

Understanding a Friend in Crisis

C risis. It's an experience that can stop people in their tracks and immobilize them. They're thrown off balance and into panic and defeat. All people want at this time is relief. The crisis hits them suddenly…or it could be the last straw in a series of negative events. People often make some of the greatest changes in their lives when they experience a crisis. They're forced to change when the way they used to solve problems doesn't work anymore. So they're looking for solutions. Your friend may see you as a solution.

What is experienced as a crisis by your friend may not be a crisis to you. You need to see it through his eyes. And to help a friend in crisis, you need to understand what constitutes a crisis.

Underlying any crisis is a loss or series of losses. Your friend won't be himself now. He will be different. It's as though someone came up and hit him over the head with a two-by-four. He's stunned. His world isn't the same any longer. His brain is in turmoil. The right side of the brain (the emotional side) has been overwhelmed, which results in an overwhelmed left side (the thinking side). And so in this state your friend reaches out to you.

What is your friend likely to want from you in this time of crisis? People's needs vary, so don't be surprised by the wide range of requests you hear. In many cases, you'll be expected to be a miracle worker. He may view you as his last hope, and his expectations can be excessive, unrealistic, or both. When you can't produce what he wants, don't be surprised if you hear disappointment or anger. Yet you *will* be able to help in ways that will meet some of his needs.

What are some of the different responses you may see from your friend?

- He may want a strong person to protect him and make decisions. "Please take over for me." (You can't.)

- He may need someone to help him maintain contact with reality. "Help me know that I am real." (This you can do.)

- He may feel empty and need love. "Care for me." (This you can do.)

- He may need a helper to be available and provide a feeling of security. And he may call you constantly. "I want you to always be here." (You can't do it. Helping is a part-time endeavor, not a full-time job.)

- He may feel obsessive guilt and be driven to confess. "Take away my guilt." (Only the Lord can do this.)

- He may feel an urgent need to talk things out. "Let me get this off my chest." (You can listen—remember the definition of true listening.)

- He may demand advice on pressing issues. "Tell me what to do." (Be careful. You can help him discover *options*.)

- He may want help sorting out conflicting ideas. "Help me put things in perspective." (You can help.)

Can you think of other needs your friend may have? In some situations, your friend may come with *all* of these, making *you* feel overwhelmed. Even though you want to help, it's good to set the boundaries you need to stay healthy.

Characteristics of People in Crisis

Of the various friends who seek your help, some will cope quite well with their crises while others cope poorly. To predict which will be which, be on alert for these characteristics.

- *Overwhelmed.* The first characteristic of people who cope poorly is that they are nearly overwhelmed in a crisis. Why? Prior to the crisis they were already struggling emotionally. Now they respond in a way that makes matters worse, but from their perspective they're doing the most efficient thing possible.

- *Poor physical condition.* The second characteristic of those who cope poorly in a crisis is poor physical condition. They have fewer resources to draw on during a crisis.

- *Hard time coping.* Those who deny reality have a hard time coping with a crisis. Denying reality is their attempt to avoid their pain and anger. They may deny that they're seriously ill, or financially ruined, or that their child is on drugs or terminally ill.

- *Magic of the mouth.* This is the tendency to eat, drink, smoke, and talk excessively. When difficulty enters these people's lives, they seem to regress to infantile forms of behavior. Their mouths take over in one way or another. Do you have any friends like this? They're uncomfortable unless they're doing something with their mouths most of the time. This attempt to not face the real problem can continue after the crisis is over. The person is creating an additional crisis.

- *Unrealistic approach to time.* People who cope this way crowd the time dimension of a problem or they extend the time factors way into the future. In other words, they want the problem "fixed" right away or they delay and delay dealing with it. Delaying avoids the discomfort of reality but can enlarge the problem. If your friend delays, be prepared for a difficult time in helping.

- *Excessive guilt.* Those who struggle with excessive guilt will have difficulty coping with a crisis. Why? They tend to blame themselves for the difficulty, and by feeling worse they immobilize themselves even more.

- *Blamers.* Blamers have a difficult time coping with a crisis. They don't focus on what the problem is but turn to "who caused the problem." Their approach is to find some enemies, either real or imagined, and project the blame on them.

- *Excessive dependence or independence.* These friends either turn away from offers to help or become clinging vines. The ones who cling tend to suffocate you. She'll call you several times a day. Boundaries have little meaning. An overly independent friend will shun your offer to help. Even if she's sliding downhill toward disaster, she doesn't cry out for assistance. When the disaster hits, she either continues to deny it or blames others.

One other characteristic must be cited that has a bearing on all the others:

- *Belief system.* A person's theology affects how he or she copes with a crisis. People's lives are based on their theology, and yet so many people are frightened by that word. Our belief in God and how we perceive God is a reflection of our theology. Those who believe in the sovereignty and caring nature of God have a better basis for approaching life and crises positively.

Phases of a Crisis

We will now look at the typical pattern that occurs in a person's life as she goes through the changes in a crisis sequence. As you can see from the chart, there are four phases in life-changing events or crises: impact, withdrawal/confusion, adjustment, reconstruction/ reconciliation.

Phases of a Crisis

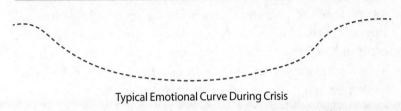

Phase 1	Phase 2	Phase 3	Phase 4
Impact	Withdrawal/ confusion	Adjustment	Reconstruction/ reconciliation

Typical Emotional Curve During Crisis

	Phase 1 Impact	Phase 2 Withdrawal/ confusion	Phase 3 Adjustment	Phase 4 Reconstruction/ reconciliation
Time	Few hours to a few days	Days to weeks	Weeks to months	Months
Responses	Choose to stay and face crisis or withdraw	Intense emotions: drained, angry, sad, fearful, anxious, depressed, guilty, rage	Positive thoughts start returning, as do all emotions	Hope returns, self-confidence builds
Thoughts	Numb, disoriented; insight ability limited, feel overwhelmed	Thinking ability impaired; uncertainty, ambiguity	Able to problem-solve again	Clear thinking
Direction to regain control	Searching for what was lost	Bargaining, wishful thinking, detachment	Looking for something new to invest in	Progress evident, new attachment made to something significant
Searching behavior	Often reminiscing	Puzzled, unclear	Can stay focused and begin to learn from the experience	Pause to evaluate where you've been and where you're going

Phase 1: Impact

The impact phase is very brief. A person knows immediately that she's been confronted with a major happening. For some people it's like being hit with a two-by-four. The impact phase involves becoming aware of the crisis and experiencing the effect of being stunned. This period lasts from a few hours to a few days, depending on the event and the person involved. In a severe loss, tears may occur immediately or a few days later. The more severe the crisis or loss, the greater the impact and the greater the amount of incapacitation and numbness. The impact phase can linger on and on, as in the case of a divorce proceeding.

During this phase the person has to make a decision whether to stay and fight the problem through to resolution or run and ignore the problem. This is called the "fight or flight" pattern. During the impact stage, your friend is usually less competent than normal. Her usual tendency of handling life's problems will probably emerge. If the tendency in the past has been to face problems, she'll probably face the problem now. But if her tendency has been to avoid problems, she'll probably run from this one.

> Be careful with your responses. If your friend senses you're feeling uncomfortable, she may shut down her feelings.

Fighting and attempting to take charge in the midst of crisis seem to be the healthier responses. Running away only prolongs the crisis. And since each of the phases is dependent on the adjustments made in the previous one, avoiding reality doesn't make for good judgment. Pain is prolonged instead of resolved.

Mental processes decreased. Thinking capability and insight ability decrease during the impact stage. Your friend may be somewhat numb and disoriented. She may even feel she can't think or feel at all. It's as though her entire system shuts down. Factual information you give your friend may not fully register at this time and may need to be repeated later on. (This is why suggestions, plans you make, and so forth need to be written down for your friend.) You may explain something to her, and then she might ask a question that indicates she never heard one word. Because she's numb and stunned, she may make unwise decisions. Unfortunately, making important decisions may be necessary. This is where she needs your help. And if you don't have the answers, perhaps you can find them or ask for help.

Searching for what was lost. During the impact phase, a person physically and symbolically searches for the lost object. Her thought process is directed toward the loss. It's common for a friend who loses a loved one to take out photographs and other items that remind her of the person who died. When something that means a great deal is lost, people hold on to their emotional attachments longer than they normally would. It's normal to search for the lost loved object, or a representative, or a replacement. The searching behavior is greater when people aren't aware of the grief process and what's happening to them.

Reminiscing about the loss is in proportion to the value of the lost object or person. Your friend needs to be listened to and have her feelings accepted at this point of the crisis. Feeling rejected delays resolution of the problem. Feelings shouldn't be buried or denied. Your friend may even feel strange about the feelings and thoughts she's experiencing. Negative comments from others won't help at all. Be careful with your responses. If your friend senses you're feeling uncomfortable, she may shut down her feelings. Instead, take the time to discover the source of *your* discomfort and deal with it. By doing this, you'll become better able to respond to life yourself and to help others.

Feelings of guilt. Guilt frequently accompanies change and crisis. People feel guilty for many reasons, from having failed to having achieved. Many have difficulty handling success. They wonder if they deserve it or, perhaps, they see others who didn't succeed and in their empathy for them experience guilt over their own successes. Children of parents who divorce sometimes feel guilty as if they were responsible for the destruction of the marriage. Those who witness accidents or catastrophes often experience guilt. "Why was I spared?" "Why did my young child die and not me? He had so many more years ahead of him than I did." These are common reactions.

A friend experiencing guilt has several choices available to alleviate guilt. She can rationalize her way out of it. She can project blame onto others. She can attempt to pay penance by working off the guilt. Or she can apply the forgiveness available through Jesus when there's been genuine sin or a violation of God's principles. God can and will remove true guilt.

There might be other feelings of guilt that have no basis. A person who lives by her emotions most of the time will be more guilt-prone during a crisis. Those who have negative patterns of thinking or self-talk will exhibit guilt more than others. Forgiveness from God isn't usually needed for false guilt. What is needed is help in changing her perspective or self-talk. She has to want to do that, and changing takes time, so it probably won't be accomplished during the short impact phase.

Note: Before we go on to the next stage, let me explain how the use of the Phases of a Crisis chart has been helpful. Often when people in crisis come to me for counseling, they feel overwhelmed and wonder, "Is my response normal?" On many occasions I've shown these people the chart, gone through the various stages, and then asked them to indicate where they were. I usually do this when they're in "Phase 2: Withdrawal/confusion." They respond by first identifying which stage they're in and then asking, "You mean my response is normal?" By discovering the normalcy of their responses (feelings), they feel relieved. And the chart helps them see where they're heading, which further alleviates their anxiety. I carry a laminated copy of this chart with me in my Bible. Feel free to make a copy and do the same.

Phase 2: Withdrawal/Confusion

Intensity in emotional levels. One of the key factors in the withdrawal/confusion phase is the emotional intensity. The shock has worn off, and the underlying feelings intensify. If you look back at the chart, you'll notice that each phase becomes progressively longer. Phase 2 can last days and even weeks.

Denies feelings. During this phase, the tendency to deny feelings is probably stronger than at any other time because now they can become ugly and very potent. Intense anger can occur toward what happened, which in some cases brings on guilt for having such feelings. Depression, sadness, fear—these are part of the denial process. Shame can then result, and the pain of the various feelings might bring the tendency and desire to suppress all feelings to the forefront. This denial, in time, leads to emotional, physical, and interpersonal difficulties. The best step you can take in helping your friend is to help her identify and put words to her feelings. Give a copy of the Ball of Grief chart to your friend, ask her to identify her emotions, and then let her know that what she's feeling is normal.

Ball of Grief
The Tangled Emotions of Grief

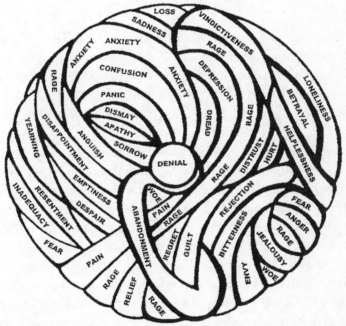

How do people feel when confronted by a crisis? What goes on in their emotional spectrum when they find it difficult to adjust to a major difficulty? Your friend may make one or more of these statements:

- "I've never felt this way before" (bewilderment)
- "I feel so scared—like something terrible is going to happen" (danger)
- "I can't think clearly. My mind doesn't seem to work" (confusion)
- "I'm stuck. Nothing I do seems to help" (at an impasse)
- "I've got to do something, but I don't know what" (desperation)
- "Nothing can help me so what's the use in trying?" (apathy)
- "I can't cope by myself. Please help me" (helplessness)
- "I need help right now" (urgency)
- "I feel so miserable and unhappy" (discomfort)

Knowing this can assist you in relating to your friend if she's having difficulty identifying her emotions. You might make statements such as, "Could it be that you just aren't thinking clearly? You feel like your mind isn't working?" "Could it be that you feel stuck and nothing anyone does seems to help?" "Do you feel immobilized, perhaps thinking, 'Why try? Nothing I do seems to help'"?

Remember, if your friend senses that sharing her feelings with you shocks and alarms you, she'll tend to repress them. But they are never repressed from God. He understands and accepts her emotional state, and He loves her always. Feelings need to be expressed, which means that friends and relatives—her support system—need to be available. Unfortunately, the availability of other friends and relatives might not coincide with when your friend needs help. Meals, gifts, cards, time, and prayers usually come during the impact phase and the beginning of the withdrawal/confusion phase. But in a few weeks after the crisis, that support system diminishes—just when it may be needed most. That is one step you can take—to assist your friend in developing an ongoing support system.

Needs support. During the withdrawal/confusion phase, your friend *does not* need or benefit from spiritual and psychological insights. Her emotional state, whether it be anger or depression, interferes with reception of the information. You can pray that she'll be able to draw on what she's already learned because she'll find it difficult to incorporate anything new at this point in the grieving process.

One of the best ways to aid your friend during this phase is to offer your help in organizing her life. She may need assistance in arranging appointments, keeping the house in order, and other routine responsibilities. People need this help because they may be suffering from some paralysis of the will because of their emotional state.

Above all, when you work with a person in phases 1 and 2, use *sustainment responses*. These are basic, simple, and what we've been talking about: listening, reassurance, encouragement, and reflection. These approaches will help lower your friend's anxiety, guilt, and tension while providing emotional support. Your task is to help her restore balance in her life.

Searches for support. Another tendency at this phase is self-pity. Your friend may appear confused and focused on what she's lost. This may be evident because she'll begin a task or start to approach people and then retreat. She may be looking for people or situations that can act as a type of replacement for what was lost. When she retreats, it's to reminisce about what she's lost.

During this phase your friend would be well advised to avoid making decisions regarding replacing or compensating for what was lost. She is not ready because she hasn't fully released whomever or whatever was lost.

Note: I use the Ball of Grief chart in two ways. One way is asking the person to identify which of these feelings she's experiencing. The second way is to ask which of these feelings she *isn't* experiencing. Once again your friend will probably ask, "You mean these are normal responses?" And you can respond with "Definitely!" Encourage your friend to take this chart out each day to help her identify what she's experiencing. Often at each appointment, I ask the person to evaluate her fear or depression or anger on a scale of 0 to 10. Eventually she'll discover that her negative emotions are decreasing. It's a helpful way to measure improvement.

Phase 3: Adjustment

Notice the length of time Phase 3: *Adjustment* takes. This phase lasts longer than the others. The emotional responses during this time start turning hopeful. Some depression may remain or come and go, but positive attitudes are starting to return. Life is looking up. Your friend may talk positively about future possibilities, such as enjoying a new job or a new location, rebuilding a fire-destroyed home, or considering remarriage. She's just about completed her detachment from what was lost and is now looking for something to replace what was lost or fill in the gap for the absence the loss caused.

> Your friend still needs someone to be close and available for support.

Climbing out. What is occurring in her world begins to take on new importance. She has been through the depths of the valley of grief and is now climbing out. What she begins to attach to holds special significance for her. Outsiders may not see the same significance and feel she's making a mistake by choosing this new job, new home, or new partner. Your friend doesn't need you as a critic. She's responding from a perspective different than yours. You need to see her life and decisions through her eyes.

The one area in which you may want to caution your friend is if she selects a new partner. At this phase that is usually too soon, whether her loss of spouse was caused through death or divorce. I encourage those who are going through divorces to wait at least a year following the divorce before dating. And it's imperative that they complete a divorce recovery program as well. Recovery needs to occur first or they'll select new partners from positions of weakness, and the baggage they bring from their previous relationships will interfere with the new ones.

This may be the time to recommend books and other resources to help your friend recover. Timing is essential, and you don't want to force this issue. (I've included several resource options at the end of this chapter.)

Allowing hope. At this time your friend will be hopeful, but it isn't a consistent or pervasive sense of hope. Her outlook will fluctuate, and she'll have down times. She still needs someone to be close and available for support. Because her insight ability is returning, she can be more objective about what has occurred. Her ability to process new information and suggestions is back. She will gain new insights spiritually at this point, and her values, goals, and beliefs may be different now and have greater depth. Now is the time to ask questions such as, "Where has God been in all of this for you?" "How has this impacted you spiritually?" "What have you learned through all of this that will help you the next time you hit a crisis?" "How have you changed?"

Phase 4: Reconstruction/Reconciliation

Spontaneous expressions of hope. Now that your friend has reached phase 4, she'll display a sense of confidence and make plans from that confidence. Doubts and self-pity are gone. Your friend has made a logical decision at this point not to engage in them anymore. She takes the initiative for progress, and reattachments are occurring. New people, new places, new activities, new jobs, and new spiritual responses and depth now exist. If there has been anger and blame toward others or if relationships were broken, this is now the time for reconciliation. Helpful gestures, notes, and meals shared together and doing helpful acts for others may be forms of reconnecting.

Reflections of newness. The final resolution of a crisis is a reflection of the newness of a person. A crisis is an opportunity for your friend to gain new strengths, new perspectives on life, new appreciations, new values, and a new or stronger way to approach life.

Surviving and Growing Through Crisis

I've experienced the four phases of a crisis in my life. Sometimes it's possible to work our way through the four phases in less time because of experienced or threatened loss. Quite a few years ago, I experienced strange physical symptoms, including vertigo, pressure in the back of my head, and headaches. These symptoms persisted for about seven weeks, during which time the doctors had some theories but nothing concrete. There was real uncertainty about my health, and my own concerns and worries about what this might be added to the feelings I experienced.

Finally, after going through further examinations, including a CAT scan, the symptoms disappeared. As the doctors and I pieced together what had occurred, we felt the physical symptoms were brought on by my conducting too many seminars with no recuperation time in between, having a cold, and the altitude changes at some of the seminar locations. Physical exhaustion was one of the greatest culprits. This experience, especially at the age of 47, caused me to think, evaluate, and consider making some changes. I didn't like what I went through, but I grew because of it and realized it had been necessary to get my attention.

This is what happens in a crisis. At this time, encourage your friend in the growth you've seen. Continue to pray for her and with her. The two of you could even talk about how your friend can use what she's learned to help others.[1]

Recommended Reading

Loss of a Spouse

H. Norman Wright, *Reflections of a Grieving Spouse*

Loss of a Child

H. Norman Wright, *Missing the Child You Love*

Pamela Vredvelt, *Empty Arms: Hope and Support for Those Who Have Suffered a Miscarriage, Stillbirth or Tubal Pregnancy*

John MacArthur, *Safe in the Arms of God*

General Help on Grief

David Jeremiah, *A Bend in the Road*

H. Norman Wright, *A Better Way to Think*

H. Norman Wright, *Recovering from the Losses of Life*

Chapter 6

Loss or Trauma?

There's a new word in our vocabulary these days: *trauma*. Oh, we've heard it before, but since the terrorist attacks on September 11, 2001, it's taken on new significance. Events in the United States have made trauma and the threat of trauma a reality for most Americans. The first major terror attack on US soil that made the news occurred in 1993 at the World Trade Center in New York. In 1995, the Alfred P. Murrah Federal Building in Oklahoma City was blown up. And, of course, there was the devastation of the 2001 World Trade Center/Pentagon/Pennsylvania terrorist attacks using airplanes.

And terrorism isn't the only cause of trauma anymore. Shootings, murders, and other heinous crimes in public seem to always be in the news these days, including the killing spree in a Colorado movie theater, the bombing at the 2013 Boston Marathon, and the violence committed at schools, airports, and shopping malls. Americans have joined much of the world in facing the daily reality of terrorism, murders, and other such evils at home.

Trauma is what we experience due to any event that shatters our belief in a safe world. It's more than a state of crisis. Trauma leaves us feeling vulnerable and unprotected. Our place of refuge has been invaded. People live with trauma right in their neighborhoods, right on their blocks. You may have experienced it. And it's certainly happened to someone you know. Just turn on the news. No one can get away from it these days.

The first man and woman on Earth, Adam and Eve, certainly experienced trauma.

Remember the story of Job? He lost his family, servants, animals, and farm suddenly and by violent means (Job 1:13-19). David had several close (and no doubt traumatic) encounters with death that involved giants, King Saul, war, and animals (1 Samuel 17:4-52; 18:10-11; 19:8). David also witnessed hand-to-hand combat and thousands of brutal murders (even ordering one that we know of—Bathsheba's husband Uriah). These events and more affected David's personality and immediate family. His daughter Tamar was raped by her half-brother Amnon (2 Samuel 13:10-18). David's son Absalom murdered Amnon because of what he'd done to Tamar, and later Absalom too died a violent death (2 Samuel 13:28-29; 18:9-15). The Bible recounts other traumas. In Judges 19 we read about gang rape. Jonah was almost shipwrecked, he was thrown overboard, and then he was swallowed by a big fish (Jonah 1–2). Jesus Christ's crucifixion on the cross was very traumatic for Him, His disciples, His family, and His followers then and today.

The word *trauma* comes from a Greek word that means "wound." It's a condition characterized by the phrase "I just can't seem to get over it." This experience isn't limited to those who have gone through war. I've seen it in a father who saw his daughter fatally crushed in an accident and in people who were sexually abused. Those who have had abortions have experienced it. I've seen it in paramedics, chaplains, and nurses. I've also encountered it in survivors of robberies, traffic accidents, and domestic violence. I heard it in the voice of my neighbor as he described witnessing an armed robbery in a video store. Trauma touches those subjected to pressure or harassment in the workplace. I've also seen it in the faces of those impacted by terrorist attacks. Perhaps you've seen it too or even personally experienced it.

You may think your friend has experienced a loss, but it could have been trauma. If that's the case, you may want to suggest he see a trauma specialist.

What Is Trauma Like?

What people used to see as a safe world is no longer safe. What they used to see as a predictable world is no longer predictable. Most people overestimate the likelihood that life is going to be relatively free from major crises or traumas. Most underestimate the possibility of negative events happening to them. Perhaps that's why we're so devastated and our core beliefs so shaken when a tragedy or trauma occurs.

What beliefs do you and your friend hold about life? What will happen to those beliefs if either of you experiences a trauma? Will they be tested? Will they survive? It's important to ask yourself these questions *before* trauma enters your life or the life of someone you know.

If someone has been feeling invulnerable and thinking, "That won't happen to me," trauma will not only wound him and shake his beliefs, it will fill his life with fear. If your friend has been traumatized, expect this. *Invulnerability is an illusion.* People don't have to be victims of terrorist attacks or mass shootings to suddenly feel vulnerable. Just viewing the vivid pictures on TV and photographs in newspapers and books are sufficient to take us from the role of spectator to participant. We end up believing, "If it can happen there, it can happen here." What were you feeling during the weeks after September 11, 2001, or after the latest shooting of innocent victims? What were your friends feeling and talking about?

> Understanding more about trauma will help you become a healing, supportive influence in your friend's life.

We see trauma all the time on TV. Crime shows, police dramas, and "reality" TV constantly show up-close details of traumatic events and results. But even these take a backseat to the real-life events reported on newscasts every day. Snatches of tragedies are shown, usually along with scenes of a memorial service, a few anguished words from a family member or victim, and then the news quickly shifts to another tragedy.

Perhaps you're asking the questions most people are these days: "How widespread are traumatic events in our country?" "How many people are exposed to traumatic events, such as natural and technological disasters, accidents, crime, abuse, and war?" Counselors used to say 75 percent of the general population in the United States has been exposed to some event that meets the criteria for being trauma producing. Now that percentage is even higher. The good news is that only 25 percent or so of those exposed to such events become trauma-tized.[1] Those who do, need help as soon as possible. Yes, people can experience a crisis and not end up traumatized. There are also people walking around today who believe that the state of trauma they're in is just the way life is. It's not. Even if you're not traumatized by an event, your friend may be. Understanding more about trauma will help you become a healing, supportive influence in your friend's life. Your pres-ence, your help in normalizing his feelings, your recommending a spe-cialist could make a difference.

Physical trauma affects people two ways. Obviously some part of the physical body is impacted with such a powerful force that the body's natural protections, such as skin and bones, can't prevent the injury. The body's normal, natural healing capabilities can't mend the injury quickly without some assistance. Perhaps not as obvious is the *emotional wound-ing* caused by trauma. The human psyche can be so assaulted that our beliefs about ourselves, our lives, our will to grow, our spirits, our dig-nity, and our sense of security are damaged. Have you seen this happen to a friend? He feels helpless and hopeless. People can experience this to some degree in a crisis and still bounce back. In trauma they'll have difficulty bouncing back because they feel *derealization* ("Is this really happening?") and *depersonalization* ("I don't know what I really stand for anymore").

Trauma's Effects on the Brain

As the result of trauma, something happens in our brains that affects the way we think, including how we interpret and store the event we experienced and the way we process information. In effect, trauma overrides our coping system and activates our alarm system. It has the power to disrupt how we process what we see and hear. When we can't handle the stress, we activate survival mode.[2]

Most of us aren't aware of what happens inside our brains during crises. There's an "alarm portion" of the brain that controls behavior. When we've been traumatized, this alarm system becomes hypersensi-tive. It overreacts to normal stimuli. For example, when a person who has been assaulted sees a large person, he may react by falsely believing,

"He's going to hurt me. Oh no!" even when the situation doesn't warrant that response. Another section of the brain is analytical and tries to calm down the emotional part of the brain. The analytical process evaluates what's going on and usually puts it into correct perspective. "No, just because that person is large doesn't mean he's going to hurt me."

Usually our body, emotions, and thoughts are connected. But in trauma it's as though the left side (the cognitive) and the right side (the emotional) of our brains get disconnected. Trauma separates them. We may have vivid and graphic thoughts about what happened but experience no emotion. Or we might experience intense emotions without realizing the thoughts or even the actions that occurred. One man said,

> "I feel like my brain was disrupted and one part is transmitting the AM and the other the FM. Sometimes there are holes in my memory like a slice was taken out. Other times I can't get those intrusive, unwanted memories to stop. I want them evicted! I can't remember what I want to remember, and I can't forget what I want erased."[3]

This will sound familiar to people who have undergone trauma. I've heard people say, "It's like my mind was scrambled."

Susceptibility to Trauma

Are some people more susceptible to being traumatized than others? If your friend is "emotionally healthy," if he came from a "healthy home," if he's a "strong Christian," is he immune to trauma? No, and neither are you. Everyone is susceptible to trauma; everyone is at risk. Our previous mental stability, race, gender, level of education, and previous emotional health seem to make little difference when trauma hits. However, our ability to handle life's ordinary stresses and our developed coping skills can help us deal with trauma somewhat.

If you or a friend becomes traumatized, it's *not* because of a defect or weakness. Strong emotions are normal responses to an abnormal event. Although your personality won't alter the outcome of experiencing trauma, the trauma *does* impact your personality. Yes, people do vary in their responses and capacity for endurance during trauma. Some people have better coping skills than others. Those who have strong faith in Jesus Christ and an accurate understanding of life truths taught in the Bible use these powerful resources to help them cope. But everyone has a "breaking point," a time when defenses get overrun.[4]

Too often when we meet someone in trauma we're threatened because we want her to be better, to be normal, to be "fixed" quickly, and we don't know what to do when it doesn't happen right away. So we withdraw or do or say something that isn't helpful.

There's one last factor to consider. People involved in natural catastrophes seem to experience shorter, less intense Post Traumatic Stress Disorder (PTSD) than those involved in human-caused disasters. If a natural disaster can be seen as an act of nature or God, people think, "That's just life." The survivors don't lose as much trust in others as do those involved in human accidents. Another word for a person-caused tragedy is *atrocity.* That's why the attacks in Oklahoma City, Columbine, New York City, Boston, and elsewhere impacted people so much. Also, those who experience one trauma usually recover more quickly than those who experience multiple traumas.[5]

What experiences qualify as traumas? There are so many possibilities. As you read the following paragraphs, consider the people you know (including you) who have experienced natural catastrophes such as earthquakes, fires, floods, hurricanes, tornadoes, volcanic eruptions, landslides, or life-threatening windstorms. For instance, I've been in threatening windstorms, been jolted out of bed by earthquakes, and when I was a teen my family was saved by our collie, who barked and alerted us to a fire in our home. Thankfully, none of these events were severe enough to traumatize me…but witnessing a train wreck did.

Sometimes there are community or work-related disasters, such as chemical spills or explosions that hit people hard. Trauma can occur in the survivors of refugee or concentration camps.

Many people become traumatized through sexual or physical assaults. In the United States, by age eighteen, 25 percent of girls and 16 percent of boys have been sexually abused. For some children trauma is going home at night. Children who were physically mistreated by excessive beatings, spankings, confinement, or deprivation of food or medical care can be seriously affected for life.

People can be traumatized by witnessing death or serious injury, by seeing a violent crime being perpetrated, or by being exposed to an uprising, riot, or war.

Children, who have less capability than adults to handle significant events, can be easily damaged. At risk of trauma is any child who has witnessed the murder, suicide, rape, or beating of a family member, significant adult, or friend. And the number of children who experience trauma from gang violence is growing.

Many of these conditions mentioned so far pertain to being witnesses. When it happens to your friend or you, it's even worse. Being a combatant, prisoner, or medic in war creates the potential for trauma. Anyone who has been robbed, mugged, abducted, raped, kidnapped, terrorized, or injured in a vehicular accident experiences trauma. Any situation in which you feel that you or another family member could be killed or hurt gives cause to experience trauma. Those involved in the helping professions, such as police and firefighters, are subject to trauma if they've been involved in just one of these conditions:

- witnessed death and injury
- experienced a threat to their own safety and life
- made life-and-death decisions
- worked in high-stress conditions

One last condition that can produce trauma is stress, such as working long hours or being in an unsafe environment. Paramedics, rescue teams, police, firefighters, and medical personnel—all are at risk of experiencing trauma.

My son-in-law, who is a firefighter, has experienced first-and-second-degree burns fighting fires. He's witnessed numerous deaths and made many significant life-and-death decisions. Firefighters frequently have to operate on very little sleep, and they often work

48-hour shifts. Overwhelming? Very possible. But this is what happens in their professions.

> Traumatized people can recover, but they need help and hope.

If you or someone you know has experienced any of these events, then you or that person has experienced trauma. This doesn't mean that being traumatized or PTSD will necessarily result, but the event has the potential to lead to it.[6]

Keep in mind that what is traumatic to one person may not be to another. You may be thinking, "I hope I don't have to try to help someone who's been traumatized." It will probably happen. We can't always choose who comes to us for help. We can choose to be there, to be present, to listen, and to pray. For many, this will do wonders.

What can you do if you're helping someone who has been traumatized? Learn as much as you can, and encourage the person to learn more. Read *I Can't Get over It!* by Aphrodite Matsakis and *Finding Hope When Life Goes Wrong* by H. Norman Wright and Julie Woodley. You can also refer people who have been traumatized to trauma specialists.

Traumatized people can recover, but they need help and hope. By listening to them and encouraging them, you can make a positive difference.

Chapter 7

The Hazards of Trauma

Trauma has many effects. It can shatter our beliefs and assumptions about life, challenge our belief that we have the ability to handle circumstances, and tear apart our belief that the world is a just and orderly place to live. That's quite dramatic, isn't it? Whether trauma hits your friend or you, here is what to expect:

- Trauma leads to silence: "I don't have the words to describe it."

- Trauma leads to isolation: "No one seems to understand the experience I had."

- Trauma leads to feelings of hopelessness: "There was no way to stop what happened, and there is no way to stop the memories of what happened."[1]

Our level of optimism crumbles. We all want a valid reason for what happened to us. We want to know *why* so we can once again take control and regain a sense of order and predictability. But in trauma we end up with unanswered questions. Your friend might say, "I always thought right would prevail, as well as justice. What happened seems so unfair!" So what do we do when we expect the good guys to always win and the bad guys to always lose—but it doesn't turn out that way? Job said it well: "If I cry out concerning wrong, I am not heard. If I cry aloud, there is no justice" (Job 19:7 NKJV).

We all want answers, expect answers, plead for answers, but sometimes heaven remains silent. That's when our faith might undergo a crisis in addition to whatever else is impacting us.

Trauma also affects how your friend sees himself, his self-identity. We all have a mental picture of ourselves, and when what we see doesn't line up, we get thrown off course. Your friend might see himself as a rational, strong, take-charge, in-control person. Trauma challenges all that.

Flashbacks

Trauma can be recurring. Thoughts, pictures, dreams, nightmares, and flashbacks of what happened may occur. Sometimes these may slip into your friend's mind like a video stuck on continuous replay. Sensitivity to the situation can become so extreme that an event can trigger such a strong flashback that she feels and acts as if she were experiencing the original trauma all over again. Surprisingly, this is normal. One firefighter from New York City said,

> After the Trade Tower disaster I heard about others who died, and it was like a carousel of faces running in front of me. There were classic pictures that will be in my head forever. I knew thirty guys who aren't here anymore. I can see them, feel them, taste them. I don't know what to make of it! There's just no language to describe what you see and feel. It's like a nightmare you can't wake up from. I see a lot of destruction but this was magnified a million times. I'm just trying to grab on to life.

In a flashback, it's as though the person leaves the present and travels back in time to the original event. It seems so real. She sees it, hears it, and smells it. Sometimes a person reacts as if she were at the original event. Your friend may be hesitant to admit this for fear of your reaction. A flashback is a cry of pain that needs to come out and does so in the only way it can.

A friend of mine, a Vietnam War veteran, often experiences flashbacks at police funerals or whenever he sees a flag-draped coffin. I've been with people who can't watch certain movies because of the effects they have on them. I've been with a person who, when the loud rumbling of a truck went by, reacted as though a major earthquake was occurring.

A combat veteran walks down a street and hears a car backfire. He dives behind a car to hide from the enemy and recalls his friends who were blown up in front of him. A victim of rape has a flashback when making love to her spouse. An accident victim has a flashback at the sight of a car wreck or blood. Someone sees an object falling from a building and once again sees people jumping from the World Trade Center.

Reminders, or triggers, can occur on the anniversary of a traumatic event. As the date draws near, the intensity of the original trauma builds. Holidays and other family events can create strong emotional responses as well. It's possible for a traumatized person to be set off by something she sees, hears, smells, or tastes. One of the high school students who witnessed a classroom shooting said when he goes hunting the smell of gunpowder sets off traumatic memories. In the case of abuse, a confrontation with the abuser may bring back emotional or physical reactions associated with the abuse.

If your friend has experienced trauma, you might consider forewarning him about the possibility so he won't be shocked if it occurs.

Even systems designed to help victims can cause them to relive the painful event. The trial system, sentencing process, police, and the mental health system can cause traumatic reactions to recur. You may need to accompany your friend to some of those meetings or encounters.

Certainly the media doesn't help reduce trauma by their graphic coverage of the worst incidents in life. Neither do movies and television shows that include extensive, graphic portrayals of violence. These depictions can bring back memories of a person's victimization.[2] Encourage your friend to avoid certain programs and to consider not listening to news media at bedtime for a while at least.

When survivors can talk about the trauma, write about it, and take it to God in an honest and real way they are dealing with their emotions instead of repressing them. This means there isn't as great a subconscious need for them to be brought forward through intrusive thoughts, nightmares, images, or flashbacks. At first your job as a friend may be to accompany your friend to a church service and let others who know and care about him that this may be a difficult time and share how they can join you in being supportive.

Sometimes a person's trauma emotions repeat not through memories or images but through *painful* and *angry feelings* that seem to come out of nowhere. These feelings occur because they were repressed at an earlier time. Now the emotions are crying out for release. If your friend blows up or overreacts, listen to him but realize the emotions aren't aimed at you. Don't take the negative reaction or words personally.

Another way your friend may re-experience trauma is through *numbing* and *avoidance*. It's painful to rehash the trauma experience. For some, it's agonizing. Your friend wants the pain to go away and disappear forever, but it doesn't so his body and mind take over to protect against the pain. This is done by emotional numbing. His defense system kicks into gear to help him adjust. When numbing occurs, it not only creates distance from the trauma, but it can also result in diminished interest in all areas of life. He may feel detached from people around him—even the ones he loves the most. Often he lacks emotional expression because he's shut everything down. He may reduce his involvement with activities and life in general.[3] Numbing is an okay short-term coping mechanism, but it becomes harmful when the person is prevented from dealing with the trauma and his emotions.

When trauma is re-experienced, your friend may feel some of the emotions he didn't experience at the time of the event because of the immediate numbing coping mechanism that kicked in. Now when feelings of rage, anger, guilt, anxiety, fear, and sadness emerge, he wonders, "Where did these come from? They hurt, and I don't want them!" so he shuts down again so he won't feel as if he's going through a series of out-of-control mood swings. And then he may avoid situations he thinks might trigger those uncomfortable and scary feelings. He might retreat from people, from family gatherings, and even from life. He could do this mentally, socially, physically, and spiritually. If this is happening, continue to reach out in a nonthreatening, gentle manner. For instance, you could sit quietly with your friend for half an hour. Can you do that? You may need to.

Your friend might stay away from the type of place where the problem occurred. If he was robbed in a restaurant, he may avoid restaurants. I've seen firefighters, police, and medical personnel seek other lines of work after they've been traumatized.

> Being traumatized is curable. Recovery is possible, but it is a slow process.

Those who have experienced trauma have their own set of triggers that can activate the memories of what they experienced. Listen and be alert to what may be triggers for your friend. Remember, he may not be aware of them.

There's something else you can expect to see in a traumatized friend. He's on edge, which is usually referred to as *hyperalertness* or *hyperarousal*. The strong emotions he experiences—fear, anxiety, anger—affect his body, particularly the adrenaline output. During a traumatic event, the heart races, breathing is labored, and muscles tighten. Some people, in an attempt to make sense of what is happening, mislabel their body's responses. They may say, "I'm going crazy," "I'm going to collapse," "I'm having a heart attack," or "I'm dying." Some never correct the way they mislabeled their physical responses. That means that anytime their hearts pound or it's hard to breathe, they misinterpret what's happening and don't realize it's from the trauma. They are experiencing a panic attack and don't realize it.[4] If you've never witnessed a panic attack, your friend's response may scare you.

For some victims of trauma, strong emotions, such as fear, rage out of control. But the flip side could also be true. I've worked with many people who were paralyzed by fear. You may have a friend like this. Sometimes he's afraid to make a decision, risk another's disapproval, or take a stand. He may be afraid that others don't like him. And, even worse, he's afraid to break out of the pattern he's trapped in.

This discussion on trauma is basic and simplified, but the information is solid. Hopefully it will help you remain alert to the fact that trauma exists and is, perhaps, closer to you than you realize. If you identify yourself as someone experiencing any degree of trauma or PTSD or you know someone who fits the characteristics, remember:

1. *Being traumatized is curable.* Recovery is possible, but it is a slow process. Your friend needs to hear this.

2. *Your friend will need to work with a professional.* Someone who is equipped to assist those experiencing trauma will be able to help your friend start on the road to recovery. This could be a highly trained minister, chaplain, or therapist.

3. *Control can come through understanding.* The more you learn about trauma for yourself or for others, the more you and the other person will feel in control.

The Other Side of Trauma

There is another side to trauma. Current research on those who have been traumatized indicates the majority of victims say they eventually benefited from the trauma in some way. And these are people who experienced as much pain as those who never fully recovered. How did they benefit? There was a change of values, a greater appreciation for life, a deepening of spiritual beliefs, a feeling of greater strength, and the building of stronger relationships.

"The most important element in recovering is to remain connected to people."[5] Your friend needs people to walk with her during this difficult time of life. One of the best steps for your friend to take is to stop seeing herself as a person who is diseased or deficient. Your friend is not abnormal because of her trauma symptoms. The *event* she experienced was abnormal. The event was so out of the ordinary that it overwhelmed her, as it would almost anyone, including you.[6]

Three Stages of Recovery

How do people recover from trauma? They go through three basic stages: *the thinking stage*, *the emotional stage*, and *the mastery stage*.

The Thinking Stage

The *thinking stage* involves fully facing the trauma, remembering the details, and sometimes reconstructing it mentally. This isn't a matter of dwelling on the past but of taking fragmented and disconnected memories and pulling them together so your friend can make sense of the present. Sometimes this stage involves talking with others (such as you), recreating the scene, or reading any available written accounts of it. When this is accomplished, she'll be able to view what happened from a new perspective—a more objective view rather than a judgmental view.[7] It'll be like reading a newspaper account.

She needs to look at what happened through the eyes of a detached observer (even though it may be difficult) rather than as an emotionally involved participant. One option is to suggest your friend write out her story longhand. (*Yes, by hand!* That's crucial.) Have her include as much detail as possible. Tell her to let the story flow without editing. In doing this, she'll drain the poison out of the trauma. This diminishes the hold of intrusive thoughts and flashbacks. She may need to repeat this process several times. (After my first three trips to New York to help people affected by the terrorist attacks on September 11, 2001, I spent three hours each time writing my story longhand. I wrote what I experienced, thought, saw, and felt in order to drain the emotions and not become "secondarily" traumatized.)

If your friend works through this stage, she'll acquire a new assessment of what her real choices were during the traumatic experience. She'll have a better understanding of how the event has impacted the totality of her life. Hopefully this will reduce any self-blame that most people experience going through trauma. Finally, she'll gain a clearer understanding of who or what she may be angry at.[8] And anger is usually present—and that's also all right.

This stage deals with the mental arena. Healing and recovery must also involve the *emotional* level.

The Emotional Stage

The next level is *the emotional stage*. It necessitates dealing with the feelings she may have repressed because of the trauma. In trauma, many of the feelings are painful, and to deal with them the emotions must be expressed at gut level. This isn't easy. Many people have a fear of feeling worse, losing control, and not being able to "return to normal." Your friend doesn't have to act on the feelings, but she does need to face them. Her emotions might include anger, anxiety, grief, fear, sadness…and the list could go on and on.[9]

How can you help? If your friend shows signs of anger, have her…

- draw or visually depict her anger
- whisper her feelings in as loud a voice as possible
- give the emotions other descriptive names
- write a letter to her anger
- have her anger write a letter to her.

You get the picture, I'm sure. The possibilities are endless.

The Mastery Stage

The final stage is *mastery*. This is when your friend finds new meaning through what she's experienced. Her perspective becomes that of a *survivor* rather than a victim. Who has the greatest potential to become survivors? People who have a solid, personal relationship with Jesus Christ and a biblical worldview.

Mastering trauma involves your friend making her own decisions instead of allowing experiences, memories, and people to make decisions for her. This is a time of growth, change, and new direction. What people learn because of trauma probably couldn't have been learned any other way. Here's what Scripture says:

> Blessed be the God and Father of our Lord Jesus Christ, the Father of mercies and God of all comfort, who comforts us in all our affliction so that we will be able to comfort those who are in any affliction with the comfort with which we ourselves are comforted by God. For just as the sufferings of Christ are ours in abundance, so also our comfort is abundant through Christ. But if we are afflicted, it is

for your comfort and salvation; or if we are comforted, it is for your comfort, which is effective in the patient enduring of the same sufferings which we also suffer (2 Corinthians 1:3-6 NASB).

I've had people ask, "How do I know my friend is growing and getting better?" First, your friend needs to develop a new way of looking at progress. It may be slow. There may be regression. She needs to focus on the *improvements* rather than on the times she feels stuck. One man told me he charted his progress each month on a scale of one to ten, as well as his entire journey of healing up to that point. That helped him better understand his progress.

> One of the delights of recovery is developing a new appreciation for life.

How can a person tell if she's progressing and moving ahead? Symptoms become less frequent, and the struggle with fear becomes less intense. One of the fears that is so disheartening is the worry of going crazy or insane. This fear also diminishes.

There will be times when the only way to get rid of anger and the desire to seek revenge is to face the fact that nothing can be done to change what happened or to prevent a similar occurrence in the future. The next step is to give up a portion of the anger or resentment each day. She can say, "Today I'm giving up five percent of my anger. Tomorrow I'll give up another five percent."

As your friend moves through her journey of recovery, the rigidity that helped her cope will diminish. She'll gradually rediscover the values of flexibility and spontaneity up to the level she's comfortable with based on her unique personality.

One of the delights of recovery is developing a new appreciation for life. Your friend will see things she missed before, hear what she didn't hear before, and taste what was tasteless before.

She'll probably rediscover her sense of humor and its healing properties. A new or deeper sense of empathy for the wounded around her will likely occur. Trauma survivors can become healers who have great compassion for others. "Weep with those who weep" takes on new meaning (Romans 12:15 NASB).[10]

As mentioned, people recovering from trauma will benefit greatly by measuring their progress. For years I've asked counselees to keep daily or weekly journals and write out in detail what they are experiencing and feeling. Some also kept a time line of their recovery, while some did both. Over time this helped make them aware of their recovery in a tangible way.

A "recovery time line" is simply a way to record the peaks and valleys of the recovery process. You can have your friend use the chart on the next page or create one like it. Use a one to ten scale, with 10 being feeling great and 1 being depressed. At the end of each day, have your friend indicate on the graph where she is for that day. Have her continue to chart her mood for as long as it takes to show her recovery. It could take months or years, but over time growth will be revealed.

Instructions: Once a day chart how you're doing emotionally. Although your emotions will go up and down, over time you should see a gradual incline as you adjust, cope, grow, and recover from the trauma.

When your friend has experienced trauma, sometimes that's all she remembers. You can help her by asking her to leapfrog over the trauma event and look at what her life was like before. What was her life like? What did she do each day? You can assist her by asking these questions and having her write down her answers in her journal.

- What was your biggest struggle back then?
- What fulfilled you?
- What did you enjoy the most?
- What did you look like? (Be very specific about this. Sometimes pictures and videos help the process.)
- Who were your friends?
- What did you like and not like about yourself?
- Who did you get along with? Who didn't you get along with?

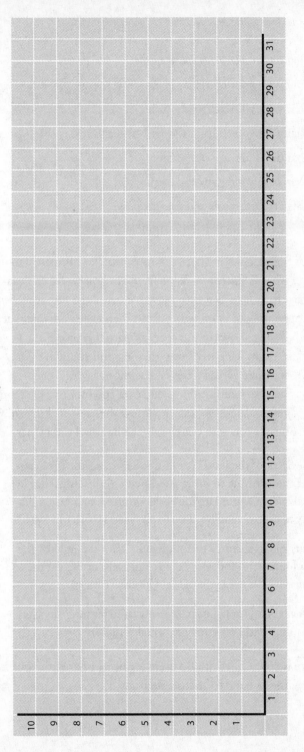

Recovery Time Line

Month: _____

- What did you believe about God?
- What were your Christian practices (for example, prayer)?
- What were your beliefs about life?
- What were you realistic about? Naïve about?
- What did you want out of life?
- What were your goals and dreams?
- What are your goals and dreams now?
- What would you like to be different now?

As your friend looks at what she wrote, help her compare it to today and decide what is different. Ask her what choices she can make to help her create the life she wants. Have her list all the things she would like to happen now (dreaming big), and then check off what she can accomplish if she chooses to pursue each particular goal.

Ask what might keep her from growing and changing. For many, it's the lack of a plan. Dreams can fade without a plan.

You may need to remind your friend over and over that overcoming trauma is a *process*, a *journey*. Let her know she's not making the journey alone. She has you and, better still, she has the Lord by her side:

> The Spirit of the Lord God is upon me, because the Lord has anointed me to bring good news to the afflicted; He has sent me to bind up the brokenhearted, to proclaim liberty to captives and freedom to prisoners (Isaiah 61:1 NASB).

> Jesus spoke again to them, saying, "I am the light of the world; he who follows Me will not walk in the darkness, but will have the Light of life" (John 8:12 NASB).

> [David said,] "You, Lord, keep my lamp burning; my God turns my darkness into light" (Psalm 18:28).

You *can* help your friend! Be there for her. Listen with your heart, reach out with the hands of Jesus, and pray.[11]

Recommended Reading

H. Norman Wright and Julie Woodley, *Finding Hope When Life Goes Wrong*

Michael Scott, *Moving On After Trauma: A Guide for Survivors, Families and Friends*

Chapter 8

Helping Your Friend

When a friend calls and needs your help, there is a "best way" to respond. First, remember you are helping as a compassionate friend. Second, in some cases, your friend may need professional help. However, you may be the first one he reaches out to, so be ready to stand in the gap for him. Keeping this in mind will encourage you to pray more and be dependent on the leading of the Holy Spirit for listening, what to say, and what to do. Some of the same suggestions will apply whether your friend has experienced a crisis or a trauma.

As you're gathering initial information from his story and his answers to your questions, you're seeking to discover: (1) which issues in your friend's life need to be attended to immediately and (2) which issues can be postponed until later. You may need to help your friend make this determination because so often people in crisis aren't aware of what can wait and what must be handled at once. Sometimes your help could be as simple as getting him some food and encouraging him to rest. As you get more experience in helping in crisis situations, you'll discover that you seldom have to conduct a question-by-question approach to find out critical information. Your friend will volunteer most of it. But as you discuss his situation with him, *be sure to keep the questions in this chapter in mind.*[1]

Be aware of your friend's level of alertness and communication capability. Identify the cause of the crisis by asking: "Tell me what happened to make you so upset?" or "Will you tell me why you're so upset? I'd like to hear about it." Getting your friend to *tell his story as he experienced it is foundational.* Don't start the conversation by asking about feelings. "Tell me how you're feeling" is *not* a good starting point.

Those in a crisis sometimes have difficulty stating clearly what they want to say. When this occurs, you'll need to be extremely patient. Giving any verbal or nonverbal indication of impatience or discomfort, such as urging your friend to hurry, is counterproductive. Allow for pauses and remain calm and interested. Especially during the impact phase of a crisis, there is a time of confusion and disorientation, and mental processes are not functioning as they normally would. Some of the pain may be so extreme that words won't come easily. In some cases, there may be no words to adequately describe your friend's experience.

Sometimes what you're hearing may not sound rational—and it may not be. How do you handle irrationality that you can't stop? Let go of your own need to be in control and embrace your desire to help others feel better. Helping a devastated friend will tap your energy and push your ability to be flexible to the wall. It's common as well as all right to wonder, *Will this ever end?* or *I don't know how much more of this I can take.* Just as your friend's reactions are normal, so are yours. Hang in there and pray for your friend and yourself.

Responding to Your Friend

As you listen to your friend, notice if there are any themes. Look for statements being repeated or moments when your friend speaks with great intensity. These are clues to her point of distress. After your friend has described what's happened, you can ask, "What thoughts are going through your mind at this time?" or "What did you think about when that occurred?" Since her thoughts are in such disarray right now, you're trying to help her focus by reducing the clutter and cobwebs. As your friend begins to think a bit more clearly (this will come and go), she will feel a bit more in control. But know that she may not remember all of what happened, and

> Bringing a sense of calm, stability, and relief to your friend will be much appreciated.

this may bother her. Details may be sketchy. Reassure her that these lapses are normal for what she's been through.

Eventually you can ask, "What was your *reaction* [or response] to this?" Especially if you're talking with a man, use the words *response* and *reaction* because many men don't relate well to the word *feelings*.

On occasion you may need to channel the direction of the conversation. Some crisis situations need *immediate* action rather than waiting until tomorrow or next week. You want to reinforce statements that are related to the crisis and avoid responding to unrelated topics, such as rambling statements that deal with the past or peripheral events. You might say, "What you've just said sounds important to you, and in the future we'll talk about it. But right now, it doesn't seem directly related to your real concern. Let's come back to that." This process of focusing helps him filter out material that is irrelevant to the crisis, although your friend may not realize what is and isn't important at this point in time. Maintain a gentle, supportive tone.

If you're confused by what is said, don't hesitate to ask for clarification. When she's able to express the issues fairly clearly, help her explore what choices she has for dealing with the situation. Ask questions such as, "What else might be done at this time?" Discover what other support systems your friend has if you don't know—spouse, family, friends, coworkers.

People in crisis interpret their environment as something that's difficult to manage. They see confusion and perhaps even chaos. If you can, help her realize a greater sense of order in her environment. Bringing a sense of calm, stability, and relief to your friend will be much appreciated. Perhaps she needs to stay at a different location for a while. She may need some space and quiet or to be away from people who are attempting to help but are actually adding to the confusion.

As your friend talks with you, assess what she's telling you and compare it to the problem as you see it. Remember, often a crisis is triggered by the person's *perception* of what has occurred. There may be times when you feel your friend is overreacting, but remember that what she is reacting to might not be the main problem. Some people fall apart over an insignificant occurrence because it's really a trigger mechanism. There may be a blocked or delayed response to another crucial problem. For example, a mother seemed to be functioning quite well after a major accident that killed one person and critically injured her son. But while washing dishes in her kitchen, she dropped a plate. She fell apart, alternating between hysterical weeping and intense anger. A relative visiting in the home couldn't understand this reaction to the simple breaking of a plate. A friend who worked with the upset woman later in the day was able to bring all the factors together.

Your Role as Caregiver

An often asked question is, "How do I know how much action to take?" A good rule of thumb is take extensive action only if circumstances severely limit your friend's ability to function. And when you do take action, you want to encourage him to move into an independent role as soon as possible.

If the crisis is likely to result in danger to your friend or to others—if he's emotionally overwhelmed and has no capability to function or take care of himself, he's on drugs or alcohol, or if he's injured—you need to take a more immediate, *directive role*.

When your friend isn't a danger to others or himself and he's capable of making phone calls, running errands, driving, and caring for himself and others, your role is *facilitative*. The two of you may create the action plan together, but your friend needs to be the one to carry it out. You may even want to work out a "contract," verbal or written, with him that details how and when portions of the plan are to be carried out.

Does all this sound like what a counselor does? Yes, but it's quite structured and you *are not* acting as a therapist. Whether you're taking directive action or a facilitative role, *listening* and *encouraging* are your primary tools. Any advice you offer should focus on helping your friend figure out *his* options. You might say, "You know, I'm concerned about what's happening to you at this time. Let's consider doing this for now…"

You can advise new approaches and actions and new ways of thinking about or looking at a situation. Often I have people come to me with statements like

"I'm cracking up."

"I think I'm going crazy."

"I must be the only person who feels this way."

"Other people don't have this much pain, do they?"

"I'm really a crummy Christian, aren't I?"

"If I had more faith, I wouldn't be responding this way."

What are these people really saying? What are they really feeling? They're saying, "I'm out of control, and I'm afraid." They're trying to figure out what's happening to them, and this is their attempt to understand their predicament.

Here's your opportunity to offer your friend realistic reassurance. Use statements such as, "It's common to feel this way; and it's doubtful that you're going crazy" and "Your reaction and feelings are normal considering all you've been experiencing." Or you might say, "With all you've been through, I'd be a bit concerned if you weren't reacting in some way." Helping him realize that his feelings and reactions are normal may provide some peace and a sense of relief.

Often I show the person I'm helping the Phases of a Crisis chart. This helps relieve his emotional pressure (see chapter 5).

I know you want to be helpful, but before you take action, ask yourself these questions:

- "Is this something my friend could—and should—do for himself at this point in time?"
- "What will this accomplish in the long run?"
- "How long will I need to be involved in this way?"

- "Are there any risks in doing this? If so, what are they?"
- "How could my friend be helped in a different manner?"

Your friend's feeling of helplessness is strong during a crisis. You can counter this helpless feeling by encouraging him to come up with alternative responses and then take action. This will also help him operate from a position of strength, of doing, rather than weakness, of just being caught in the circumstance. One way to help is to ask how he's handled previous difficulties. This reminds him there are steps he can take and helps him look for alternatives. Remember to let him—not you—do as much of the brainstorming and action work as possible to rebuild and strengthen his self-esteem.

Coach him to consider the possibility that there are more alternatives or choices. Some of your statements can be structured in an open-ended way: "Let's consider this possibility…" "What if you were to…" "What might happen if you…" "Let's think of a person you feel is a real problem-solver. What might that person do?" Be sure to help your friend anticipate obstacles to implementing the plan he comes up with. Otherwise he might get derailed when he encounters the first bump in the road. And don't assume he'll follow through without encouragement and checking in later.[2]

One way you can assist is by helping your friend avert catastrophes and move toward a state of balance. For instance, if he's just lost his job you can encourage him and help him make a list of his qualifications, abilities, and job experiences. The simple task of completing a positive action step may provide stress relief and positive motivation.

Since most people in a crisis or trauma feel hopeless, it's important to *foster hope* and *positive expectations*. Don't give false promises, but encourage your friend to solve his problems. Your belief in his capabilities will be important. This is a time when he needs to "borrow" your hope and faith until his own returns. Let him know through your actions that you expect the crisis to be resolved in some way at some time, you expect him to work to solve the problem, and you're willing to help him as much as you can. Your approach and interaction with your friend conveys this better than making a blanket statement to him in a conversation.

The problem-solving approach is a positive step and much better than giving false reassurances. On occasion it's helpful to ask about past crises and upsets to discover how he handled them successfully. If you're familiar with some of these, you can refer to his handling of them. This will help him see that he's been able to work through problems. This will help instill hope for handling the current problem.

Assist your friend in setting goals for the future if he's at that phase in the crisis sequence. As his anxiety level drops, he'll see the situation in a more objective manner. When this occurs, he can reflect on what has happened and what is now occurring. Don't be surprised when his laughter returns. There is "a time to weep and a time to laugh," as the third chapter in the book of Ecclesiastes tells us. Humor allows us to take a break from the heaviness of loss or tragedy. Many people in the helping professions use *gallows humor* to handle the pain and tragedy they deal with on a continued basis.

You can help your friend restore balance in his life in several important ways. First, look at the information he's giving to you about the situation. Does he have all the facts? Is he distorting the situation because of his emotions or bias? Does he understand that certain responses and feelings are normal during a time of crisis?

Asking pertinent questions and prodding for informational answers will let you (1) help him fill in some informational gaps and (2) help him understand his fears and concerns can be diminished by receiving accurate information. Both steps are moves toward restoring equilibrium.

How well does your friend grasp the choices of action open to him in light of the recent changes in his life? What options are open to him (such as caring for the children if his spouse has died or left)? Anyone in a crisis situation needs help considering the choices and consequences of decisions both to himself and others who may be impacted. Examining choices and consequences and then selecting a path enables him to cope now and will help him in future situations.

As your friend gains greater strength and capability, he'll be able to examine his part in the situation and analyze his own responses.

Providing Support

What else can you do? You can provide support. One of the reasons a problem may develop into a crisis is a lack of an adequate social support system. Intervention in a crisis involves giving support. Initially you may be the only one giving it! Even being available to talk by phone is a source of support.

The knowledge that you're praying for your friend each day and are available to pray with her over the phone is another source of support for her. Don't be surprised by the number of "urgent" calls during the early steps of a crisis. Your friend is saying she needs to gain support through contact with you. These calls need to be returned promptly, but that's not the same as immediately. If you drop everything you're doing to call back, a dependency relationship could be developing. If you wait a half hour before returning the call, your friend has an opportunity to do some thinking on her own. She may calm down. By the time you talk to her, the problem or issue is no longer critical or she's come up with a solution. This is important because it takes you out of the miracle-worker role.

People in crisis need the assurance that they can call you at any time, and you are willing to talk to them for a few minutes. Will this work for you? What about your own work and family? You may decide your friend needs to see a trained pastor or counselor while you play a secondary, supportive role. But even if you tell her to call anytime, she may still struggle with whether or not to call. If you don't let her know she can call, her struggle could be intensified and, therefore, add to her crisis condition.

> Friendship is a calling, a privilege, and a blessing.

At some point you may need to set limits on the phone calls as your friend becomes better able to handle her life. (That in itself is one way to express limits.) Because you can tell she's better able to handle what's occurring, you can ask her to exercise her capabilities a bit more.

The best way of supporting your friend is to encourage her to expand her support system as soon as possible. This reduces demands on you, helps her through the immediate crisis, and might help prevent a crisis in the future.

Determine what type of support system your friend has. Does she have relatives or friends in the area? Are they healthy and well-functioning or will they drag your friend down or add to the chaos? Your friend needs supporters who replenish not deplete. Whom has she told about her difficulty?

Learn about the helping agencies in the area—financial, housing, suicide prevention, counseling center—so you can direct your friend toward such help when needed. Neighbors and friends may be able to provide babysitting or transportation if needed. People from her church might provide cooked meals for a specific period of time. Help your friend determine whom she can draw on and what those people can do to reduce the pressures on her during this time of crisis. This is a very practical way of helping.

If appropriate, be sure you give specific guidance to the support people. Ask them not to give a lot of advice, which may be well intended but unnecessary and further muddle the situation. Sometimes you may need to give direct guidance even though it will seem uncomfortable. But whoever said helping a friend would always be easy? It costs time and energy, but it's worth it. Friendship is a calling, a privilege, and a blessing.

Chapter 9

When Depression Hits

I'm not sure what to do for this friend. Every time she calls she's either depressed or worried sick. I know she's been through a lot recently, and I wish she'd get some help. I'm not sure what to say or do, and I don't want to make the situation worse." Most of us find ourselves in this quandary sometime. You may be the first link in helping your friend find the help she needs.

First, depression is a very normal response to loss and trauma. If your friend is depressed, she desperately needs someone to help her. Unfortunately, she may not be able to effectively communicate what she's experiencing. If you haven't felt hopeless and helpless yourself, it may not be easy for you to understand what she's going through. You may feel frustrated because of her inability to fully explain what she's going through. You also might get frustrated because you want to help but don't know what to do.

Picture your depressed friend down in a deep pit. The pit is dark, cold, and very isolated. Your friend is frighteningly lonely. On all sides there are only sheer rock walls with no handholds or solid footholds that would provide a way to climb up and out. Your friend in the pit is completely helpless and easily becomes resigned to darkness and despair. She sees no way of escape.

This is how your friend feels when she has sunk to the depths of depression. She feels overwhelmed and imprisoned by nagging and potentially deadly feelings of worthlessness, fear, and self-blame. Concerned friends or family members stand above on the edge of the pit, yearning to help. Even so, it's very hard for the person in the pit to call for help because of the paralyzing feeling of helplessness. Sometimes the person even has a difficult time admitting to others that she's down there.[1]

> When your friend has no hope, you can loan her your hope until she regains her own.

As you go to help your depressed friend, pray for understanding and patience. You'll need an abundance of both. Your offer of assistance may be rejected at first, and it could be some time before it is accepted. You can't just go down into the pit, grab her, and hoist her to the top. You'd like to, but life doesn't work that way. Your friend must be willing to trust God and the people in her life. She must decide to climb out of the pit herself and be willing to take the first steps. Your encouragement will be like a ladder placed inside the pit, and it might give her the motivation and hope to begin the climb.

Picture yourself at the top of the pit looking down. There's a balcony at the top, and you're leaning over the railing cheering her on. Your belief in her ability to climb out may be the source of strength she needs right now. When your friend has no hope, you can loan her your hope until she regains her own.

You can also help the depressed person capture hope through the Word of God:

> Do you not know? Have you not heard?
> The Everlasting God, the LORD, the Creator of
>   the ends of the earth
> Does not become weary or tired.
> His understanding is inscrutable.
> He gives strength to the weary,
> And to him who lacks might He increases power.
> Though youths grow weary and tired,
> And vigorous young men stumble badly,

Yet those who wait for the LORD
Will gain new strength;
They will mount up with wings like eagles,
They will run and not get tired,
They will walk and not become weary
(Isaiah 40:28-31 NASB).

If you're around a depressed person, you'll need to protect two people—the depressed person and yourself. Why? Because your friend's depression will affect both of you. You're dealing with someone who is very sensitive right now, and you must exhibit a certain sensitivity toward her too. You're the giver and your friend is the receiver. Even if you're okay with helping, you may still feel a bit irritated or angry by the way she's acting. This, in turn, might make you feel guilty for feeling that way. Because of your emotions, you may respond in ways you don't want to or intend, which may increase your stress. Your friend will sense your tension, and she might feel even worse because she feels she is a burden on you. With all the emotions swirling around, you may feel drained too.

If you're depressed, don't attempt to help someone else with depression or you'll become overwhelmed. Your relationship will experience additional strain as well.

What can you say to a friend going through depression? A simple statement like this works great: "I care for you, and I'm available to listen, to talk, to be fully present. I want to help you and be with you." Put your arm around your friend or hold her hand. There is healing in nonsexual physical contact. A touch on the shoulder, a pat on the back, or holding an arm conveys acceptance and "You're not alone. I am with you." Be honest and say, "I don't understand all you're going through, but I'm trying to understand. I am here to help you."

You may never know what praying with and for your depressed friend accomplishes, but you can rest assured that it has far-reaching benefits. In a time of depression when your friend has lost hope, you can lend her your strength and hope to carry her through. When she's lost faith, she needs your faith to sustain her until hers recovers.

Practical Guidelines

Most people don't know what to do for a depressed person. Here are some practical suggestions. How closely you follow these will depend on the intensity and duration of the person's depression and your relationship. If he is depressed for only a few hours or a day or two or if he is feeling down but is still functioning adequately, not all the ideas will apply. But if the depression has lasted for weeks or months, your friend is dragging and not functioning well (not eating or sleeping), apply the appropriate measures.

1. *Understanding the causes and symptoms of depression is the first step toward helping.* If your friend is so depressed that he stares into space, ignores greetings, or turns away from you, remember that he doesn't want to act that way. In depression, the person loses some of the ability to govern his thinking and emotions. If he is severely depressed, he can't control his emotions any more than you could walk a straight line after twirling yourself around in a tight circle twenty-five times. If you understand how your friend is feeling and why he's acting the way he is—that his behavior is normal for a depressed person—then you can moderate your own responses accordingly. This will enable you to help him while keeping yourself on an even keel.

2. *Watch for self-harming behavior or suicidal talk.* Any hint, statement, or allusion to suicide needs to be talked about. I know it's difficult to accept that your friend would really consider this, but it does happen. It happened to me, so I know the devastation it can cause. Help the depressed person bring his feelings out into the open. Don't be afraid to talk about suicidal thoughts. Make sure he knows that people are aware of his situation and can be called on for help and support when needed. Ask him to tell you about any suicidal thoughts or plans. Remember too that women make many more attempts at suicide than men, but men are more likely to succeed. A divorced man over the age of forty is at the highest risk of succeeding. The older the person is, the higher the risk of success. Any person who is depressed and talking about the utter hopelessness of the future might be considering suicide.

3. *Encourage your friend to see a doctor or counselor.* If he doesn't have one, your family physician might be able to recommend someone. The time factor is very important. Don't let your friend's depression go on and on. Encourage him to do something. Even if he keeps putting you off and refusing to go, make the arrangements, guide him firmly into the car, and get him there!

4. *Identify the extent of your friend's depression.* Use a diagram like the following to encourage your friend to be honest about where he's at. Ask him to indicate with an "X" where he is at this moment in his depression. As you continue to help your friend, periodically have him evaluate his depression using the chart and note any positive progress.

0			5		10
Not depressed	A few clouds	The sky is overcast	Rain is pouring	It's flooding	Depressed and drowning

5. *Give your friend your full support.* His immediate family ought to be made aware of the situation, but be cautious about what you share without permission. When you do share, you can give them a copy of this book if they'd like specific information on how to help (also check the Recommended Reading at the end of this chapter). If possible, advise family and friends to put off confrontations or difficulties with the depressed person until he achieves greater stability. Ask the helpers to be extra gentle by not bringing up failures, coming down hard on him, or giving him challenging projects or work.

6. *Maintain contact. Don't avoid your depressed friend.* You don't want to further isolate your friend or let him perceive you don't want to be with him. That would make his depression deepen. That doesn't mean you can't set healthy boundaries if you feel overwhelmed. Some people might avoid the depressed person because they're afraid they might be the cause or a contributor to his depression. Although a person may contribute to another person's problems from time to time, no one is responsible for another person's unhappiness.

7. *Understand that your depressed friend really hurts.* He is experiencing pain. Don't suggest he doesn't really feel "that" bad or that he's just trying to get sympathy. Don't say, "Just pray about it and read God's Word more. That will solve everything." Often a depressed person ends up focusing on portions of Scripture that reinforce feelings of loss and unworthiness. If you want to offer specific verses, select them with great care.

8. *Empathize rather than sympathize with your friend.* Sympathy reinforces feelings of hopelessness. It may make him feel more helpless and affect his already fragile self-esteem. Statements such as, "It's so awful that you're depressed," "You must feel miserable," and "How could this happen to you? You're usually so upbeat" rarely help.

Remember that a depressed person's complaints are really expressions of emotional pain. Don't get embroiled in a battle over the content or type of statements. Stick with discussing *feelings.* Here are some specific guidelines for addressing common statements:

- "I'm all alone."

  Don't say: "No, you're not. I'm sitting here with you right now. Doesn't my friendship mean anything?"

  Do say: "I know you're feeling alone right now. Is there anything I can do to help? I'm glad to be here with you. Together we'll get through this lonely feeling."

- "Why bother? Life isn't worth living. There's no point in going on."

  Don't say: "How can you think that? You have two beautiful children and a great job. You have everything to live for."

  Do say: "I know it feels that way to you right now, but I want you to know that you matter to many people. You will get through this hopeless feeling."

- "I'm dragging everyone down with me."

  Don't say: "No, you're not. You see I'm fine. I had a good day today. And, besides, I'm doing everything I can to help you."

  Do say: "I know it feels that way right now. And, yes, at times it's difficult for people, but we will get past this burdened feeling together. A lot of people, including me, care about you."

- "What would it be like if I weren't here anymore?"

  Don't say: "Don't talk crazy! What's wrong with you?"

  Do say: "There are many people, including me, who would miss you terribly. You're important to so many. We'll all help to get you through this."

- "I'm expendable."

  Don't say: "If you felt better about yourself, you wouldn't say stupid things like that. God loves you and that should be enough."

  Do say: "I know you're feeling worthless right now, but we'll get through this."

- "Nothing I do is any good. I'll never amount to anything."

  Don't say: "What are you saying? You're highly respected in your career. You're blowing everything out of proportion."

  Do say: "I know it's upsetting when things don't work out the way you want them to. Feelings of failure are really painful. We'll get through this together."

- "How long am I going to feel this way? It feels as if I'll never get better."

Don't say: "Come on, nothing lasts forever. You know better than that."

Do say: "I know it's scary to be in so much pain. Feelings come and go. We'll get through this together."[2]

9. *If your friend loses interest in activities he normally enjoys, you can gently remind him of the enjoyment he derived from the activities before and firmly encourage him to get involved.* Don't ask him if he would like to participate because he might not know or care enough to respond. Don't get angry and insist, "You're going with me because I'm sick and tired of you sitting around feeling sorry for yourself." Instead, be encouraging. "I know you haven't been feeling well, but I believe you deserve some enjoyment. I think you might like this once we get there. I'd like to do this activity with you."

Another suggestion is to call and let him know when you're doing something and casually invite him along. "I'm going shopping, and I'd like to have someone with me. You know I rely on your good advice." Any activity, including window-shopping, a social event, or visiting people, is a good opportunity to invite your friend. By getting involved, your friend begins to break the destructive behavior pattern and negativity he's dealing with. This also helps him gain energy and motivation.

One of the best things you can do for your friend is help him stay busy. Physical activity while in severe depression can be more beneficial than mental activity. Help him schedule his days—by the hour works well—and include the activities he enjoyed in the past. Help him with any preparations necessary and provide plenty of details and encouragement.

10. *Gently let your friend know if he's letting his appearance go downhill.* Don't just hint about the situation. Openly, clearly, and explicitly tell him he'll enjoy getting dressed and ready for the day and may even feel more energized.

11. *Don't tease or lecture your friend about his lack of confidence.* Loss of confidence and self-esteem are common in depression. Don't ignore

the situation. Help your friend deal with it by showing him how illogical his self-disparagement is. Don't do it by berating or arguing or telling him he's being ridiculous. Instead, emphasize his past achievements and get him to focus on what he *accomplished* prior to the onset of the depression. At this point you're working with him so he can overcome feelings of helplessness.

Don't join in his self-pity. When he makes disparaging remarks, respond by saying, "Perhaps you can't do some things the way you did before, but let's talk about the things you are doing well. What do you think they are?" If he says, "I can't do anything," gently name some of the things he can do or draw them out of him through conversation. Be persistent and steady in doing this. At this point you have more control over your emotional responses than he has over his, so be very encouraging.

By following these eleven principles, you'll fulfill the biblical teaching on giving encouragement and empathy to others. "If any person is overtaken in misconduct or sin of any sort, you who are spiritual [who are responsive to and controlled by the Spirit] should set him right and restore and reinstate him, without any sense of superiority and with all gentleness, keeping an attentive eye on yourself, lest you should be tempted also" (Galatians 6:1 AMP, brackets in original). Another verse puts it this way: "We earnestly beseech you, brethren, admonish (warn and seriously advise) those who are out of line [the loafers, the disorderly, and the unruly]; encourage the timid and fainthearted, help and give your support to the weak souls, [and] be very patient with everybody [always keeping your temper]" (1 Thessalonians 5:14 AMP, brackets in original).

Dealing with Worry

There will be times when your friend struggles with worry. In fact, it will help to ask, "Do you have a tendency to worry?" Most depressed people will say, "Oh yes!" or "It's a constant battle." If the person does worry, here are some helpful ideas. They *do* work!

Read Psalm 37:1-7 aloud to your friend. You might share this too. Psalm 37:1 begins, "Do not fret," and those words are repeated later.

The dictionary defines *fret* as "to eat away, gnaw, gall, vex, worry, agitate, wear away." In addition to telling us not to fret, Psalm 37 gives us positive substitutes for worry. First it says, "Trust (lean on, rely on and be confident) in the Lord" (verse 3 AMP). Trust is a matter of not attempting to live an independent life or to cope with difficulties alone. It means going to a greater source for strength.

Verse 4 says, "Delight yourself also in the Lord" (AMP). "To delight" means to rejoice in God and what He has done for us, to let God supply the joy for our life.

Verse 5 (AMP) says, "Commit your way to the Lord." Commitment is a deliberate act of the will. It involves releasing our worries and anxieties to the Lord.

We are to "be still and rest in the Lord; wait for Him" (verse 7 AMP). This means "to submit in silence to what He ordains, and to be ready and expectant for what He is going to do in our lives."[3]

Ask your friend to read this passage and the insights out loud several times a day as a reminder to not worry. Also ask what would assist him in applying each principle to his life.

The Index Card Worry Method. This suggestion is a bit different: Say to your friend, "Tomorrow when you begin to worry about something, instead of worrying at that moment, write down what you're worried about on an index card and keep the card in your pocket. Each time a worry pops up, write it on the card—but choose to not worry about it yet. Then around four o'clock, go someplace where you can be alone. Sit down, take out the card, and worry as intensely as you can for thirty minutes over the items. Start each day with a new blank card and do the same thing."[4]

The most helpful approach I've learned over the years is the *"Stop/ Think Approach."* Suggest to your friend that he take a blank index card and on one side write the word STOP in large, bold letters. On the other side write the complete text of Philippians 4:6-9:

> Don't worry about anything; instead, pray about everything; tell God your needs, and don't forget to thank him for his answers. If you do this, you will experience God's

peace, which is far more wonderful than the human mind can understand. His peace will keep your thoughts and your hearts quiet and at rest as you trust in Christ Jesus. And now, brothers, as I close this letter, let me say this one more thing: Fix your thoughts on what is true and good and right. Think about things that are pure and lovely, and dwell on the fine, good things in others. Think about all you can praise God for and be glad about. Keep putting into practice all you learned from me and saw me doing, and the God of peace will be with you (TLB).

It's interesting to note that *God says He will guard our hearts*, but *we are to guide our minds*. Ask your friend to keep this card with him at all times. Whenever he is alone and begins to worry, he can take the card out, hold the STOP side in front of him, and say "Stop!" aloud twice with emphasis. Then he should turn the card over and read the Scripture passage aloud twice with emphasis:

Taking the card out will interrupt your friend's thought pattern of worry. Saying the word *Stop!* further breaks the automatic habit pattern of worry. Reading the Word of God aloud becomes the positive substitute for worry. If he's in a group of people and begins to worry, he should follow the same procedure only do it silently.

This suggestion may sound a bit different, but it has worked for thousands of people I've helped.

Recommended Resources

H. Norman Wright, *A Better Way to Think*, especially chapters 10 and 11.

Ellen McGraw, *When Feeling Bad Is Good*

Robert Hirschfield, MD, *Forms of Chronic Low-Grade Depression*

Donald P. Hall, *Breaking Through Depression*

A.B. Curtiss, *BrainSwitch Out of Depression*

Stephen Ilardi, PhD, *The Depression Cure*

Chapter 10

Helping a Suicidal Friend

I never want to talk with someone who is considering suicide. I wouldn't know what to do, and what if I say the wrong thing?" This statement reflects what most of us feel. What can we do or say to help someone in such dire straits? Many people who are considering suicide *call* a friend, a church, or an emergency hotline for assistance. The procedure I'm suggesting focuses on how to help when someone calls, but these principles can also be used when speaking face-to-face with someone who reveals suicidal thoughts or intentions. These are the guidelines I share with ministers and counselors when I'm called to crisis and trauma situations, such as school and community shootings.

Step 1: Establish a Relationship, Maintain Contact, and Build Rapport

For many people arriving at suicide is a *gradual* process while under stress. They seek solutions to their problems and try an alternative…then two, three, four, five alternatives without success. Then they arrive at suicide as an option. Many struggle against this choice by seeking even more alternatives, but if their way is blocked, they turn to suicide.

It's important for you to use the word "help" frequently in different contexts so the person is assured you care.

Suicidal people are ambivalent toward life and death. They wish to kill themselves because they're tired of what's going on in life. They're living in *despair* rather than hope. At the same time, they want to be rescued by someone. If an individual indicates he is suicidal, it's important to develop a *positive* relationship. This relationship may become the temporary reason your friend decides to stay alive. When you receive a call like this, you can say something like:

- "You did the right thing by calling me."
- "I'm glad you called."
- "There is help for you."

Statements like these are important because they assure the person that he made the right decision and that someone cares. Your approval communicates that he can make more good (right) decisions. He needs you to talk calmly and confidently. You want to be a voice of authority (avoid being authoritarian) in such a manner that he will not feel challenged. Caring, acceptance, and genuine concern are very important to convey.

As you talk, it's important to find common ground between you and the suicidal person. A good place to start is the fact that he has a problem and wants help, and you want to help him. Sometimes when a person is unclear and ambivalent, it takes more work to discover common ground. It's important for you to use the word "help" frequently in different contexts so the person is assured you care. It's also important to show interest in him and attempt to discern his feelings. A relationship of *trust* needs to be developed. This can be done by giving straightforward answers to questions he asks.

Step 2: Identify, Obtain Information About the Person, and Clarify the Problem

First, listen to the person's story with as few interruptions as possible. Then you can let her know that you care and that you've heard her. You can say something like, "A person in your situation is usually hurting. What hurts?" Encourage her to tell you:

- What has led her to where she is now.

- What is bothering her right now.

- What has she tried before to cope with this situation.

Remember not to challenge what she says in response to your questions. You may be tempted to do this. Statements such as "Things aren't as bad as they seem" and "You shouldn't feel that way" are setbacks to the person. They don't help.

As you read this, you're probably looking for a guaranteed approach—something that you can count on that's foolproof for reaching this person and turning her away from suicidal thoughts. But it doesn't exist. You may do everything perfectly, and it still may not work. But sometimes just your being there is all it takes to give hope to a person and take suicide off the table.

Identify the Problem

Your goal after letting her know you're supportive and you care is to obtain information to identify the person's problem. Keep her talking. Ask as many questions as you can, but avoid "why" questions. Remember, if a person is talking, she is not taking her life.

When obtaining information, you don't want to provoke her. Therefore, if what you're saying through questions or statements appears to annoy or agitate her, go in a different direction. It's better to retreat and try again than continue on and aggravate the situation. Here are some good informational questions to assist you. Even though you may already know this information because this is someone you know, ask these questions anyway. It's important for your friend to formulate answers.

- "What has happened in your life to bring you to this point?"

- "What's been going on in your life the past three months?"

- "What would need to be different for you to go on with your life?"

- "What would you need to help you?"
- "What would you like help with at this time?"
- "What would you like me to know about you?"
- "What would you like me to understand about you?"

Also keep in mind the three highly descriptive words of a suicidal person—and they all begin with the letter "H":

- *Hopelessness.* Those who kill themselves are those who have lost *all* hope. Therefore, whenever you work with a suicidal friend or coworker, do whatever you can to build in her as strong a component of hope as possible.
- *Helplessness.* A concomitant of hopelessness is often helplessness.
- *Haplessness.* Many suicidal people have had incredibly sad lives.

Obtain Information About the Problem

Suicide is a form of communication. D-I-R-T is a great anagram to use to help identify the risk factors:

D—*Dangerous.* The greater the danger in the attempt, the higher the current level of risk that the suicide is going to occur. A person with a gun is more likely to be successful than a person with a knife.

I— *Impression* (of the degree of risk). If one person believes that the suicidal person could die because of what she did to harm herself during the attempt, then the present level of risk is still high.

R—*Rescue.* If the chances were good that the person would be rescued or if she assisted in her own rescue in any way, then the present level of risk is lower.

T—*Timing.* The more recent the attempt, the higher the current level of risk.

When you talk with someone who is thinking about suicide, don't ask, "Why would you want to do something like that?" Instead, begin your assessment by asking, "How would you harm yourself?" The answer to that question will let you know quickly if the person has a plan in place. That's critical information.

As you talk, focus on what she's feeling and assist her in clarifying her feelings. If she has difficulty expressing her feelings, help her label them. Using "The Ball of Grief" can help (see chapter 5). Reflect back to the person what you believe she's thinking and feeling. This will help her pinpoint the problem. The person's overwhelming helplessness can now be broken into specific problems, which means solutions might be seen more easily. Help the person see that her distress may be impairing her ability to assess the situation accurately. When she can see the actual problem, she can begin to construct a specific plan for solving them. And if you understand the nature of the problem the person is trying to cope with, you can understand more about her strengths and weaknesses. You want to explore her reasons for wanting to die.

> Suicide should be discussed in an open and non-moralistic manner.

If a friend or neighbor calls and talks about being down or depressed, statements and questions such as these may help you pinpoint the severity of emotion:

- You seem to be depressed much of the time.
- How much have you been depressed over the past few weeks?
- When do you get depressed?
- Have you ever thought that life isn't worth living?
- Have you thought of ending it all?

These statements may help a hesitant person put her feelings into words. The actual threat of suicide needs to be out in the open for you to be able to help the person. When someone has trouble talking about suicide, she is usually relieved to find that you're not afraid to talk about it openly. At times this can relieve the person of having to hide her trapped feelings. Suicide should be discussed in an open and non-moralistic manner. Suicide is *not* a moral issue for the suicidal person. For the most part, it is the result of stress. Suicidal people are usually already struggling with guilt, and if a discussion of suicide as an immoral act occurs, it can add to the person's burden and cause further discouragement.

Does it help or hurt for you to bring up suicide? Many counselors feel it lessens the probability of an attempt by defusing the intention. You may feel uncomfortable bringing it up, but your willingness to talk about it encourages the person to be more open about her thoughts. Here are some more questions you can ask:

- I appreciate your willingness to talk with me about this. I'm wondering if there are others you want notified about what you're contemplating.

- What would you like me to tell your family and friends?

- Do you want them just to be notified or would you like them to come and see you at this time?

- They'll probably ask me questions. What do you want me to say?

- They'll want to know your reasoning for wanting to do this. What should I say?

- Before I do that, here's a different question for you to consider. You're probably thinking it's best not to be around anymore. What do you think will be better about it?

Also, don't be afraid to ask questions regarding the aftermath of her proposed suicide:

- Will anyone miss you? (Be prepared for this response: "No one.")
- If the answer is "no one," ask, "Tell me how certain you are about that—70 percent? 80 percent? 100 percent?"

- Tell me about a time in your life when people would miss you if you were gone. Who were they? What has changed? Who do you want to miss you now? What could turn this around for you at this time?[1]

Clarify the Problem

A number of factors are involved in evaluating whether a person is a high risk for suicide. As you listen to her, you'll be receiving pieces of information that will assist you in making this determination:

1. *Age and sex.* Suicide success rates rise with age, and men are more likely than women to follow through. Older single males are more vulnerable.

2. *History of suicidal behavior.* It is important to determine if this is the first attempt or if this is one in a series of attempts. The more recent the onset of suicidal behavior, the better the chance to prevent it. Yet at the same time, the need is greater for active intervention. An extensive pattern of suicidal behavior will require long-term therapy from professionals.

3. *Evaluate the suicide plan.* Look for three parts:

    a. How lethal is it? When a person has admitted planning to end her life, you can ask, "How are you thinking of killing yourself?" Sometimes the harsh words can bring home the reality of the situation. Shooting and hanging are considered the most lethal methods; barbiturates and carbon monoxide poisoning are second. The lethality of a method is measured by how abruptly the point of no return is reached. Other common methods are explosives, knives, poisoning, and drowning.

    b. How available is it? If a gun or bottle of pills is at hand, the risk is greater. Ask what kind of pills are available to the suicidal person and where they are. If she plans to use a gun, ask, "Do you have a gun? Where is it? Do you have bullets for it?"

c. How specific is the plan? If the person has worked out the details very well, the risk is higher. If the person says, "I have 100 pills here, and I am going to turn on the gas. I have covered the cracks around the door and windows so the gas will stay in," then the suicide most likely is planned and serious. If the person says she has to go out and buy the pills, or the gun, or a hose for the car exhaust the risk is lower.

Even if you're talking with a person who has a well-worked-out plan, she still called, which indicates that a small seed of desire to live remains. If the person calling is in this situation and won't say who she is (or if the person has already started the process of taking her life), you may need to work out a system of getting the attention of someone else to get help while you're talking. That person should notify the police, who will trace the call.

A person having a specific, lethal plan for suicide should sound alarms within you. If the situation is that serious, don't attempt to handle the problem by yourself. A responsible family member, a family physician, or a professional counselor needs to be included in the intervention.

4. *Stress.* This must be evaluated from the caller's point of view. To you the caller's situation may not seem significant, but to her it is. If the person has experienced losses, reversals, or even successes, it could be creating stress or strain.

5. *Symptoms.* What are the symptoms in this person's life? Is there depression? Alcoholism? Drug abuse?

6. *Resources.* What resources does this person have available to help her? Are there friends or relatives nearby? Are counseling services available in the community or at work?

7. *Lifestyle.* What is the person's lifestyle? If it is unstable, such as a history of changing or losing jobs, changing living locations, drinking, impulsive behavior, or so on, the risk of suicide is higher.

8. *Communication with others.* Has the person cut herself off from other people, including friends and family? If so, the person could be at higher risk. If she is still in touch with others, you can use them to help.

Step 3: Formulate a Plan to Help

It's important to find out what part of the suicide plan the caller has put into action so you can help him reverse his course of action. If the person has turned on the gas and sealed the windows, have him immediately turn off the gas and open the windows while you talk. *Don't let him promise to do it when you hang up.* Give specific instructions and stay on the phone while he carries them out. If the person has a gun, have him or her unload it. If it is an automatic, have them take the bullet out of the chamber and then take the bullets out of the clip. Next, have him place the bullets in a drawer and put the gun somewhere difficult for him to get to in a hurry. If he has pills, ask him to flush them down the toilet. If he doesn't want to reverse the plan, continue talking until your relationship is built to the point that he is willing to trust you or you've gotten the attention of someone who can call the police.

Once you've built this trust, get a commitment from the person. Ask him to promise to call you if he has any other difficulty or if he's tempted again to take his life. Professional counselors have found this is quite effective. The person may let other obligations go, but he will keep his promise to you.

Remember, your words of encouragement on the phone may keep him alive.

Determine Positive Resources and Alternatives

Help the person determine positive resources and alternatives he can use or do. If he's committed himself to you and agreed not to do anything life-threatening, help him widen his view of the problem to uncover more resources that he may have lost sight of during the crisis. Perhaps some other people can help the individual as well.

Create a Committed Environment

When you see the suicidal individual in person, it may be helpful to have him or her sign an anti-suicide agreement. Even though it is just a piece of paper, the person may feel more committed to following the guidelines because he signed it.

In this type of counseling, it's important to convey to the person that you care and are committed. It is also important to carefully work in the fact that God cares, as does His Son, Jesus Christ. In some cases you may feel led to say this during the first telephone conversation. At other times it may be best to say it when you meet face-to-face. Whenever you decide to share, be careful that your approach and tone don't take on a preaching air. The truth of God's love should be explained naturally and honestly, following the direct leading of the Holy Spirit at the right time.

Communicate Your Intentions

The following three elements are crucial to the phone counseling approach discussed so far:

1. *Activity.* The person needs to feel that something is being done for him right now. This assurance can relieve his tension.

2. *Authority.* The counselor must set himself up as an authoritative figure who will take change. The caller is not capable of taking charge of his life at this time, so someone else must step in.

3. *Involvement of others.* If the caller realizes that others are

now involved and caring for him, he will be more apt to feel the care and concern and will more likely respond.

Guidelines to Help the Family After a Suicide

This is one of the other situations that we hope to avoid. What can we do and say to those family members who have lost a loved one to suicide?

- Listen carefully to their questions, then answer truthfully. It's not only important to remain consistent in *your* answers, but to have others convey the same message.

- Be open about talking about the person who died.

- All of the children involved need to be told about the suicide, even the youngest ones (according to their level of comprehension).

- Encourage the children to share their feelings and questions with those they trust. Teach them to be selective about sharing the facts of the suicide.

- They will grieve better by seeing adults cry and crying with them. They need to know that crying is an acceptable and natural release for grief.

- Be sensitive to some possible feelings of guilt. Assure them that the suicide was not their fault.

- Be sure to discuss constructive ways of handling problems. They need to hear that suicide is a permanent solution to a temporary problem, and problems can be solved. Even if a family member chose suicide, the children have other options.[2]

When families respond. Consider the impact of suicide on those remaining. Just as a suicide can devastate individuals, the impact on a family (the complex web that includes brothers, sisters, parents, uncles, aunts, and cousins) can be monumental. Some families are blown apart by the guilt and blame that can follow a suicide. Some are drawn together, rallying to support one another as they struggle through their individual and collective grief and confusion. Other families continue on in silence, pretending as best they can that nothing has happened or that the suicide was an accidental death.[3]

How a surviving wife or husband reacts depends a lot on the condition of the marriage and the circumstances of the suicide. Most often survivors feel guilty for not having prevented the suicide. They also feel rejected and/or abandoned. Even if their relationship was a good one, the suicide is likely to be interpreted as something of a referendum on their married life. The surviving spouse may also feel shame, fearing that others will look on him or her as having been so awful to live with that the spouse was driven to suicide.[4]

Parents are left wondering what they did wrong. Were they too strict? Were they not strict enough? Were they too attentive? Were they not attentive enough? Even parents of children who are well into adulthood before dying wonder, *Was I a bad parent?*[5]

What to Say and What Not to Say

What can you do (and encourage others to do) to help the family and friends of a person who has committed suicide? At this more than any other time, they need the support, love, and concern of their relatives and friends. Perhaps your greatest ministry will be with the survivors. This will include close and distant family members as well as friends and coworkers. The following from Harold Ivan Smith describes their lives at this time:

> Some survivors of suicide weave well-rehearsed questions—we might call them "why's"—into the fabric of their life narratives. To know a person as a survivor is to know of the suicide that has changed their lives, although not necessarily by its details. Some survivors divide life into two segments: *before* the shadow of death, and *after* the shadow, so that a suicide is the definitive moment of their essence.
>
> Some survivors weep or wonder their why's into pillows, journals, chat rooms, shot glasses, syringes, pills, work,

sex, busyness, and religiosity, seeking relief from the stalking Accusations that menace their days, the indictments that terrorize the nights: "If *only* I had…perhaps, I *should* have…" Some will go to their graves exhausted from wondering, "Why?" or "WHY!!!!?," from asking what more they could have done, or said, or been that would have prevented the upheaval of their narrative.

Suicide, like a tsunami, rearranges the emotional shoreline forever.

Suicide alters the stories we tell others about ourselves, and the stories we tell ourselves. Sorrow is a constant companion.

A few wonder what kind of husband or wife, mother or father, brother or sister, you are, you were, if a loved one took their life.

From friendships to faith, suicide changes everything. Survivors must negotiate the altered landscape of relationships, and no relationship is immune to the effect of this death. Conversations can be laced with glances that warn, "No trespassing." Some survivors are not sure what they believe anymore. Or what they can believe: God? Heaven? Grace? Prayer? Hell? Angels? All the familiar spiritual comforters are challenged by suicide, just as bridges and high-rises in California are challenged by earthquakes, and must be checked for damage immediately after they occur.

Most especially, our connection to the one who has died suffers unexpected changes. We may find ourselves amazed when we speak words of disbelief:

> "I never thought he would go through with it…"

> "I never thought it would happen in our family…to me…to us."

> "There must have been something more that I could have done, or said, or been, or given, or…"[6]

How would you feel as a survivor? Often survivors feel completely isolated. Their basic needs are for kindness and caring. With time and the understanding and concern of their friends, as well as possibly a support group, the survivors' feelings of grief will lessen. Keep in mind that suicide is not a comfortable topic, and many people tend to forget the survivors of a suicide death sooner than the survivors of a non-suicidal death.

What is the role of the church and church members?

> The church should function as a spiritual MASH unit for survivors, helping them recover so that they can return to the battle. However, within two years of a suicide, at least 80 percent of the survivors will either leave the church they were attending and join another or stop attending church altogether. The two most common reasons for this are: (1) disappointment due to unmet expectations and (2) criticism or judgmental attitudes and treatments.[7]

Those in the congregation are survivors of suicide as well. A congregation needs support, and this is a time to address loss, grief, suicide, and how to respond to those who have been affected. Consider this: What would you do to help if one of your staff took his or her life? It happens. The following suggestions apply both to the time immediately after the suicide, including the funeral, and for as long as necessary afterward:

- Make an extra-special effort to go to the funeral home, and encourage others to do so. The shock, denial, and embarrassment are overwhelming for the survivors. They need all the support they can get. Often the coffin is left closed due to the cause of death.

- When going to the funeral home, do as you would normally do at any other type of wake. It will not be easy since you sincerely want to comfort the bereaved people but really don't know what to say. Just a few words, such as:

"This must be such a difficult time for you," "Please accept my deepest and sincerest sympathies—my heart goes out to you," and "I wish I could do more for you at this difficult time" can be a help. When you approach the people, take their hands, hug them, and don't feel the need to say anything. It's your presence that counts.

- Remember that survivors tend to become more paranoid than the average person. Why? Guilt and shame. The guilt is so overwhelming, and when people do not attend the funeral or send a card, the guilt increases. All sorts of thoughts run through the survivors' minds. A note, phone call, or visit in the weeks and months to come is a must.

- Don't try to comfort the survivors by saying, "It was an accident—a terrible accident." They're not sure. Some may think this is helpful, but it's more of an expression of the speaker's anxiety.

- Don't say, "Oh, he was on drugs or drunk. He wasn't really aware of what he was doing." You weren't there during the suicide, so how could you possibly know? It's not helpful or necessary to give reasons for the suicide. Talk with the survivors about what to say and how to respond when they hear these types of comments.

- Remember that with this kind of loss, the grief is so painful that sometimes it is easier to deny that the suicide ever happened. You need to be patient and understanding. Sometimes the denial gives survivors a break from the pain before reality sets in.

- Avoid saying that the suicidal person wasn't in his right mind or was insane or crazy. The majority of people who commit suicide are ambivalent and tormented. Even if a mental disorder is involved, that is up to someone else to determine at a later time. Telling the survivors that the person was insane may create worries of inheriting mental illness. Suicide is not inherited.

- Surviving family members and close friends have every right to feel sensitive. Unfortunately, there will be some people who deliberately avoid the survivors. They will cross the street or pretend that they didn't see them. This adds to survivor grief and guilt. Such actions are not done out of malice but rather out of confusion about what to say. It's important to make every effort to befriend the survivors and to reach out on a continuous basis.

- Accept the fact that vicious and cruel remarks will sometimes be made, even in church. They hurt survivors deeply. If you hear of any of these remarks, confront the issue and try to help the originators of the remarks realize the hurt they're causing those grieving.

- When you talk with the family, avoid discussing the signs of suicide. It's not helpful because the suicide is already a fact. Telling them, "There must have been signs indicating depression" only lays more guilt on them.

- The anniversary of a suicide is a very painful time. Relatives and friends should make every effort to be available, listen, call, visit, send a note, and do other thoughtful acts for the family.

In summary, be alert to the needs of the people impacted by depression, suicidal thoughts, and suicide. For the most part, suicidal people reveal they are considering killing themselves; therefore, be equipped and prepared. The greatest help you can give hurting people is you—your concern, your interest, your listening ear, and the love of Jesus Christ reflected through you.

Recommended Resources

David B. Biebel and Suzanne L. Foster, *Finding Your Way After the Suicide of Someone You Love*

Earl A. Grollman and Max Malikow, *Living When a Young Friend Commits Suicide*

Rita Robinson, *Survivors of Suicide*

H. Norman Wright, *Experiencing Grief*

For Pastors and Counselors

H. Norman Wright, *The Complete Guide to Crisis & Trauma Counseling*

H. Norman Wright, *Helping Those in Grief*

Harold Ivan Smith, *A Long-Shadowed Grief—Suicide and Its Aftermath*

Chapter 11

Say It in Writing

If there is anything that helps a hurting person more than spoken words, it is written words. I know. Following the death of our son we received many written expressions of comfort. And this went on for ten or eleven years—and that's what helped so much. We were very fortunate in that we continued to receive written words of comfort. Most people don't.

Most people who are hurting receive an abundance of cards and notes immediately after the crisis or tragedy. And during that time their pain is so great that words of comfort may not register as much as they will later on. I encourage you to write reminders on your calendar to send notes to the people grieving every three or four months for at least two years. This sends a tremendous message: "Your loss is not forgotten." And letters and cards don't need to be limited to responding to a death. They can be for any loss.

You want to acknowledge your friend's loss and indicate that, to some degree, you share in her pain.

Perhaps the most important part of sending a note is to put it in your own handwriting. A typed note or one purchased that you sign only doesn't convey the same message as one in your own handwriting. These are far better than a text or an email. Time after time I've heard people comment on how meaningful the handwritten notes were. Handwritten notes convey how much you care for your hurting friend. With the advent of computers, texting, smart phones, and e-cards, you may believe that handwriting a letter is no longer even viable. Or you may believe that since you seldom write, your handwriting isn't legible and your friend will have an easier time deciphering a text message. Even today a handwritten note carries a special message that your heart has been touched and you care. If you use a store-bought card, always include a handwritten comment or note.

Writing letters and notes to a hurting friend isn't easy. In fact, for many the most challenging letter to write is one of condolence. How can you craft a simple expression of words that will penetrate your friend's pain of loss and grief and bring support and care to his heart and mind? Sometimes the written word gets through more than spoken words. Many condolence letters are kept by the recipients and reread for years.

You may think, *I just don't know what to say in a letter*. Most of us don't. It's a struggle, and it's uncomfortable. We don't want to be superficial, or stilted, or come across as insincere. So we postpone writing the notes until we think it's too late to reach out that way. But if you listen to your feelings of compassion and care, you'll find writing is not so difficult after all. Your task is to translate how you're feeling into words. Your message can be simple and straightforward. You want to acknowledge your friend's loss and indicate that, to some degree, you share in her pain.

"I don't know how to put what I'm feeling into words," you say. That's all right. Few of us do. With practice it does get easier. One of the easiest ways to get inspiration if you're stuck is to go to a store and look at several appropriate condolence cards. Then simply write in your own words what was shared in those cards. Someone else's words can stimulate your own thoughts.

Guidelines for Creating Condolence Letters

The following will give you some structure if so desired. You can alter anything of them to make them more appropriate to who you are, to your friend, and to the situation. These guidelines can apply to a loss of any kind—death, divorce, breakup, and so forth.

The first component of a condolence letter is to acknowledge the loss. You don't have to beat around the bush or be subtle, but be tactful. If someone other than your friend informed you, let her know how you learned about her loss. If the loss was a person, mention him or her by name. You can share your reaction—say you were shocked, or stunned, or taken aback by the news and acknowledge your friend's possible reaction as well.

> Dear Samantha:
>
> I was taken aback today when John called to tell me that your father died last week. Dan's death was so sudden, and it must have been a shock to you too.

Next express your concern. Let your friend know that you care and that, in some way you connect with her sense of loss. If you know the person who died (or left), share your sadness. When you do this you're letting your friend know she's not alone. And use the real, appropriate words. If it was a death, use the word *death*. If it was a betrayal or a suicide, use those words. Don't try to be clever or subtle.

> It's hard to find the words to convey my love and concern for you over the untimely death of your father. I wish I could help fill that empty spot you have in your life at this time. I'll miss him too, as well as the ongoing stories you always recount to me after visiting him.

It helps to make note of the special qualities of the person who died. This can be done whether you knew him personally or just through stories from your friend. Acknowledge the attributes you felt were positive—personality, the ways he related to others, his hobbies. In doing this, you're reminding your friend that the person she lost made a contribution and was appreciated.

I remember the times I spent time with you and your father.
He was a gracious man and showed interest in what I was
involved in. He made me feel like I was part of your family. And he shared so well for a man! You and I have joked
about that before.

If possible, it helps to share a special memory you have involving
the one who died. This may help your friend since her shock and grief
may have temporarily short-circuited her ability to remember details.
When you share your memory, include what made it special to you. It
can be serious or humorous.

I remember one time when you invited me to a barbecue,
and your dad served porterhouse steaks. Remember what
he did to them? They turned into charcoal when he got distracted. His sense of humor about it and his willingness to
buy more instead of getting upset impressed me so much.
He really was a special man.

In addition to memories, you might mention special qualities
about your friend too. This is a time when she's so overwhelmed and
nonfunctional that she may question her own capabilities. "How will I
ever get through this?" "How will I ever survive?" are common expressions. Your friend needs your reassurance, your encouragement, and
your confidence. In a sense, you're loaning her your faith and hope
and confidence since her own may be sublimated by grief. You can see
what she can't at this particular time in her life. Bring out the traits that
helped her deal with past adversities that might apply now. And if you
can remember any words or affirmations the deceased made about your
friend, she needs to hear those now too.

This is going to be a difficult journey for you, but it's not the
first one you've been on. I've seen your strength and determination during adversity before. I remember your dad
saying you were not only a survivor but also a person who

could take difficult times and use them for your growth
and to bless others. In time that will occur again.

Part of your letter will be to offer assistance to your friend if you're
able to do so. Whatever you offer, be sure you can follow through.
Don't say, "Let me know if there's anything I can do." It's hard for your
friend to think specifics, let alone to ask for help. Take the lead and suggest two or three specific tasks you could do for her, such as shopping,
running errands, mowing the lawn, cleaning, or making phone calls.

> I want to help you in the best way possible. I have some
> ideas, so I'll call Saturday after you've had some time to
> think things through. We can talk about what I can do to
> help then.[1]

When you close your letter do so with a thoughtful word or phrase.
This is another time to reflect your feelings. There are many expressions you can use:

> My affectionate respects to you and yours
>
> Our love is with you always
>
> You are in my thoughts and prayers
>
> You know you have my deepest sympathy and my love and
> friendship always
>
> We share in your grief and send you our love
>
> We offer our affectionate sympathy and many beautiful
> memories
>
> My thoughts are with you now, and I send you my deep-
> est sympathy
>
> We all join in sending you our heartfelt love[2]

What about sharing your own grief experiences? This can be done if you've had a similar loss experience, but don't compare the two. The worst and most anger-producing phrase we can use is "I know exactly how you feel." No, you don't. None of us do since grief and loss are so very personal. You can, however, share the depth of your pain and how you survived:

> I remember how difficult it was to cope when my dad passed away two years ago. I'm so sorry you're going through that sorrow.

Future notes don't have to be long. In fact, they can be brief and to the point.

> Hi, James, I was having my prayer time and you came to mind. How are you really doing today? I hope you're eating and sleeping. I'll call later this week and maybe we can go out for breakfast. Thinking of you, Norm.

Share the Word of God

When you find yourself struggling with what to say, Scripture verses such as these are helpful and meaningful. But remember, Scripture alone might not reach his heart. He needs your tangible presence and thoughts too.

> The eternal God is your Refuge, and underneath are the everlasting arms (Deuteronomy 33:27 TLB).

> When you go through deep waters and great trouble, I will be with you. When you go through rivers of difficulty, you will not drown! When you walk through the fire of oppression, you will not be burned up—the flames will not consume you. For I am the Lord your God, your Savior, the Holy One of Israel…Don't be afraid, for I am with you (Isaiah 43:2-3, 5 TLB).

[Jesus said,] "Do not let your hearts be troubled. You believe in God; believe also in me…" (John 14:1).

I am convinced that neither death nor life, neither angels nor demons, neither the present nor the future, nor any powers, neither height nor depth, nor anything else in all creation, will be able to separate us from the love of God that is in Christ Jesus our Lord (Romans 8:38-39).

Even though I walk through the valley of the shadow of death, I fear no evil, for You are with me; Your rod and Your staff, they comfort me (Psalm 23:4 NASB).

God is our refuge and strength, a very present help in trouble (Psalm 46:1 NASB).

[The LORD] heals the brokenhearted (Psalm 147:3 NASB).

God has said, "Never will I leave you; never will I forsake you" (Hebrews 13:5).

My body and my mind may become weak, but God is my strength. He is mine forever (Psalm 73:26 NCV).

These two things cannot change: God cannot lie when he makes a promise, and he cannot lie when he makes an oath. These things encourage us who came to God for safety. They give us strength to hold on to the hope we have been given. We have this hope as an anchor for the soul, sure and strong (Hebrews 6:18-19 NCV).

Do not fear, for I am with you; do not be dismayed, for I am your God. I will strengthen you and help you; I will uphold you (Isaiah 41:10).

Trust in the LORD with all your heart and lean not on your own understanding; in all your ways submit to him, and he will make your paths straight (Proverbs 3:5-6).

When I pray, you answer me and encourage me by giving me the strength I need (Psalm 138:3 TLB).

Be strong and courageous, do not be afraid…for the LORD your God is the one who goes with you. He will not fail you or forsake you (Deuteronomy 31:6 NASB).

Quotations Can Help

Personal notes that include quotes, selected with sensitivity and the specific person in mind, take a little extra time and thought, but the healing effect they may have on a grief-stricken friend is well worth the effort. Sources for short, comforting quotes are almost limitless. One little book full of words of wisdom that will turn weakness into strength is *When Sorrow Comes*, by Robert Ozment. Here's a passage from that book that has been shared with those in despair:

> I wish I had a magic word to wipe away your tears! I do not know any magic words, but I know a God who can heal you and I commend Him to you. Remember, the door of death is the only door that leads to the Father's house. He will be waiting there to greet and welcome His children.[3]

Peter Marshall, the legendary Scottish chaplain of the United States Senate in the late 1940s, died at age forty-six. Uncanny as it seems, he was reported to have spoken words befitting his own eulogy: "The measure of a life, after all, is not its duration, but its donation." When the death of a younger person occurs, these words may be appropriately incorporated into a personal note.

Quotes included in notes do not have to be spoken by famous people. The main criterion is that the quote is something that helps soothe the hurt caused by the death of a loved one.

An elderly widow shared an old poem explaining that a friend copied it from a wooden decoupage at the home of another widow. These widows always pass this poem on with the hope that it will offer comfort to a new widow just as it spoke to them in their grief:

The lights are out
In the mansion of clay;
The curtains are drawn,
For the dweller's away;
He silently slipped
O'er the threshold by night,
To make his abode
In the City of Light.

Helen Steiner Rice had a special gift of expressing emotions felt by grieving persons. Books of her poems are in most libraries.

There are times when you can include poems, quotes, or Scripture. At other times prayers are appropriate to use in your letters or notes. Here are some examples.

When the joy of living is lost, O God, and life becomes a long weariness, kindle again the light that has failed, and the love that will not let me go.[4]

Lord, when sometimes my life in this world seems too much to bear, help me to claim Your wonderful promise of victory over tears, death, sorrow and pain. I thank You that all things are made new through You and that I will share in Your kingdom.[5]

I am empty, Father. I am bitter, even toward You. I grieve, not only for the one I have lost, but for the loving part of myself that seem to have died as well. You, Who have at other times brought the dead back to life, revive my dead ability to love, to be close, to care about this world and those I know. I believe, I insist, that You can heal this mortal wound.[6]

Sample Letters

The following sample letters may assist you in creating your own. The first was read in the movie *Saving Private Ryan*:

Dear Madam,

I have been shown in the files of the War Department a statement to the Adjunct General of Massachusetts that you are the mother of five sons who have died gloriously on the field of battle. I feel how weak and fruitless must be any word of mine which should attempt to beguile you from the grief of a loss so overwhelming. But I cannot refrain from tendering you the consolation that may be found in the thanks of the republic they died to save. I pray that our Heavenly Father may assuage the anguish of your bereavement, and leave you only the cherished memory of the loved and lost, and the solemn pride that must be yours to have laid so costly a sacrifice upon the altar of freedom.

Yours very sincerely and respectfully,

A. Lincoln

Letter from an adult to an adult:

Dear Wendy and Spencer,

The news of your mother's death, while not unexpected was nevertheless a blow. The final word is so definite always. I want to express my deep sympathy, but also, I feel a quiet understanding that your beloved mother—who suffered long—has finally found release. I can only imagine what the loss means to you and the rest of the family. You can all take great comfort from the fact that each and every one of you did everything possible—far beyond the call of duty to make your mother's last troublesome days as easy for her as possible. She loved her family and knew that they loved her.

Dorothy's friends know how extraordinary a woman she was as a wife, as a mother, as a friend, and as a coworker. She has left her mark on us and we know that we have lost a great friend whose life was a pattern to guide us and an inspiration to live by. May God comfort you and ease your pain.[7]

Letter from an adult to a child:

Dear Jimmy,

Today I heard that your dad died just a few hours after the terrible accident. You feel awful and like your world turned upside down. All of us feel sad because your dad was such a neat man. He meant so much to us too.

Your life will be different in the next few weeks and months. Sometimes sadness makes us feel angry and confused. All of you in your family really need one another's love. It may be hard but it helps to talk about your sadness. It may help to draw or write about your feelings.

We all love you very much. I will call you really soon.

Letter upon the death of a spouse:

Dear Kim,

For the past day, my thoughts have been of nothing but you and the beautiful Julia. I don't know if there's anything that can be said to soften the pain of your grief just now, but my love, my unqualified friendship, and my prayers are with you.

Julia was such a vibrant spirit. Her exuberance made life around her a constant adventure. You joined her on that adventure with all your heart, whether sailing through the islands or sitting silently by a mountain stream. There was a sense among many who knew you that you each embraced fully the unknowable mystery that is life. I guess the mystery just gets deeper.

I'm reminded of a short piece by Henry Van Dyke. It's called "A Parable of Immortality":

> I am standing upon the seashore. A ship at my side spreads to the morning breeze and starts for the blue ocean. She is an object of beauty and strength, and I stand and watch until at last she hangs like a speck of white cloud just where the sea and sky come down to mingle with each other. Then someone at my side says, "There she goes!"
>
> Gone where? Gone from my sight...that is all. She is just as large in mast and hull and spar as she was when she left my side and just as able to bear her load of living freight to the place of destination. Her diminished size is in me, not in her. And just at the moment when someone at my side says, "There she goes!" there are other voices ready to take up the glad shout, "Here she comes!"

So, Alex, may the winds of life blow gently around you at this difficult time. I want to help in any way I'm able. I'll call Thursday.

In trust and friendship. [8]

If the loss was traumatic in some way you may struggle with what to say. Grief is intensified if there was no opportunity to say goodbye. No goodbyes happen in the case of accidents, fatal heart attacks, homicide, or suicide. Often when a death occurs in this way there is an intensity of feelings that can include regrets, guilt, shame, anger, or rejection. There is the reaction of shock as well as the feeling of senselessness.

The following is a letter to the parents of a young woman who was murdered:

> Dear Dr. and Mrs. Rodriguez,
>
> It is with feelings of profound distress that we heard the very sad news of your daughter's death under such tragic

circumstances. Her untimely passing is a most severe and grievous loss. There is no sense to it on Earth; we can only look to Jesus, Our Lord. "Cast your cares on the LORD and he will sustain you" (Psalm 55:22).

We want to express our own deep sadness. Perhaps no words that we say will ease the pain, anguish, or emptiness that you feel in your hearts, but we want you to know that we will remember your daughter as a graceful, loving and open-hearted girl who brightened the neighborhood with her smile.

It may seem impossible now, but while nothing will ever bring Eileen back, we hope that one day you will find a source of comfort in beautiful memories of the years of joy God gave you together.

May God bless you and keep you.[9]

When my retarded son, Matthew, died in 1990 at the age of twenty-two (mentally he was about eighteen months old), my late wife and I received an outpouring of cards and letters from scores of people. We kept them because they contained so many significant memories. Since Matt lived at a special facility for the disabled the last eleven years of his life, some of the letters came from those who cared for him. Many contained a special experience they had with Matthew that we didn't know about. These experiences gave us new insights as well as memories about him, which have become very important even though to most people the experiences might seem trivial. To a bereaved parent every experience becomes special. I was comforted and felt loved by those who wrote. Their expressions assisted me with my own expression of grief, for I felt the loss more sharply each time I read a note.

In many of the letters the writers expressed their feelings and often similar experiences. Let me close this chapter with portions of several letters we received:

Dear Norm and Joyce,

I sit here this evening thinking of you and crying for you. I know the pain you feel at this time and I hurt for you. Words do little to help right now but I hope you can take comfort in knowing that Matthew is with the Lord now and one day you'll be with him again at the feet of the Lord.

All of our thoughts, love and prayers are with you.

Dear Norm,

I just heard this morning of the death of your son, Matthew. I want you to know of our personal grieving for you and our prayers for you and your family during this time. My wife and I had a son who drowned almost eight years ago, and so I can somewhat identify with the sense of loss that you are feeling. Please rest assured of our continued support and love for you as a Christian brother.

Dear Norm and Joyce,

Thank you for letting us know that Matthew has gone home to be with the Lord.

Our hearts are saddened for you as we know a little piece of your heart seems to be missing with Matthew's death— but we send our sympathy and love, hoping to help fill that hole a little bit.

Dear Dr. and Mrs. Wright,

I am so sorry to hear of the death of your son, Matthew. My wife and I lost a daughter about two years ago. And my wife has a brother with Down's syndrome who's thirty-seven, so in a couple of respects I can identify to some degree with your grief.

Unfortunately, too many in the world don't understand the joy a mentally handicapped child can bring, even when the child has grown into adulthood. And so I would imagine not everyone really knows how much you must be missing Matthew.

Dear Norm and Joyce,

You have been in our thoughts and prayers a great deal this week. We're praying you will feel God's peace and special care for you.

We have been thinking about Matthew too. Remember the time, many years ago, when we Talbot students came to your home for a Christmas party? We met a tiny Matthew, just a few months old, and as far as any of us knew, a perfect baby. And now he is perfect!

Chapter 12

Praying for Your Friend

With the ring of the phone one morning I found myself speaking to a thirty-two-year-old man who was concerned about his forthcoming marriage. As we talked he told me wanted to marry this woman he'd been going with for more than a year. He'd made a commitment and given her a ring, but now fears stemming from his childhood had begun to emerge. (This is not an uncommon situation.)

We continued to talk about the marriage and normal concerns that most individuals have concerning this major life step. "I feel I need prayer at this time," he concluded. "Would you seal our conversation with prayer?" And at that moment, distanced by many miles yet very close because of the phone connection and our common relationship with Jesus Christ, I prayed for him. I asked for God's insight, direction, clarity of thought, leading, and peace to invade this brother-in-Christ's life.

We don't have to be face-to-face to minister to a friend in prayer. As we speak over the telephone to those who are close to us, our prayers draw them closer to relying on the Lord instead of on themselves or us.

As I get to know counselees in my office, I share with them during the first or second session that as part of my counseling ministry, I pray for them each day. I also tell them I would appreciate them letting me know from time to time what they would like me to pray about in their lives so that I can be sure to be current. Many of them are taken aback that someone would remember them in prayer. Over the years many counselees have said that knowing one person was praying for them kept them going. I admit there are days when I don't pray as I've promised, but overall I'm consistent in this practice.

Praying accomplishes several things. It releases our friends to God, and it reminds us that we are not the ones who are the best Resource in this life. We need the direct intervention of God in the lives of our friends to guide, sustain, and comfort them. I've discovered that by keeping a list and praying for my counselees' specific concerns and issues, when they walk into my office I remember what their concerns were the week before. Praying reinforces their situation in my mind. Sometimes counselees ask, "How did you remember what we discussed? I don't ever see you taking notes." My answer is that praying for them is a great reminder.

There will be times when you will be stumped as to how to help, as I have been. You won't know how to proceed or what to say. It is perfectly all right to admit that. You can say, "I'm not sure where to go next or what is more pressing. Let's just stop for a moment. I'd like to ask God for guidance and insight for the direction needed at this time."

The core of helping others is prayer, but too little is said about prayer within counseling, and too little is written about its use during the session and between sessions.

This is not a chapter on what prayer is or how to pray according to this pattern or that pattern. Numerous books have been written on those topics. What I want to address is the use of prayer as a means of healing in the process of helping someone.

Scripture and Prayer

Scripture teaches that as we pray, we know we are welcomed into God's presence:

> Let us draw near with confidence to the throne of grace, so that we may receive mercy and find grace to help in time of need (Hebrews 4:16 NASB).

Blessed be God, who has not turned away my prayer, nor
His lovingkindness from me (Psalm 66:20 NASB).

When we pray, we can call upon the Holy Spirit to guide us.

In the same way the Spirit also helps our weakness; for we
do not know how to pray as we should, but the Spirit Himself intercedes for us with groanings too deep for words;
and He who searches the hearts knows what the mind of
the Spirit is, because He intercedes for the saints according
to the will of God (Romans 8:26-27 NASB).

Pray in the Spirit on all occasions with all kinds of prayers
and requests (Ephesians 6:18).

When we pray, we do so with confession, praise, and thanksgiving.

If we confess our sins, he is faithful, and just and will forgive us our sins and purify us from all unrighteousness
(1 John 1:9).

Blessed be the God and Father of our Lord Jesus Christ,
who has blessed us with every spiritual blessing in the heavenly places in Christ (Ephesians 1:3 NASB).

Be filled with the Spirit, speaking to one another with
psalms, hymns, and songs from the Spirit. Sing and make
music from your heart to the Lord, always giving thanks
to God the Father for everything, in the name of our Lord
Jesus Christ (Ephesians 5:18-20).

Give thanks to the LORD, for he is good; his love endures
forever (Psalm 118:1).

One of the important principles of prayer is to rely upon the promises of God:

Ask and it will be given to you; seek and you will find;
knock and the door will be opened to you (Matthew 7:7).

Seek peace and pursue it. For the eyes of the Lord are on the righteous and his ears are attentive to their prayer (1 Peter 3:12).

If we ask anything according to [God's] will, he hears us. And if we know that he hears us—whatever we ask—we know that we have what we asked of him (1 John 5:14-15).

Know that the LORD has set apart his faithful servant for himself; the LORD hears when I call to him (Psalm 4:3).

There may be times when you read a number of Bible passages with your friend to discover the truth of God's Word. You can use portions of Scripture as a model for prayer.

For those who are suffering:

Blessed be the God and Father of our Lord Jesus Christ, who according to His great mercy has caused us to be born again to a living hope…In this you greatly rejoice, even though now for a little while, if necessary, you have been distressed by various trials, so that the proof of your faith, being more precious than gold which is perishable, even though tested by fire, may be found to result in praise and glory and honor at the revelation of Jesus Christ (1 Peter 1:3,6-7 NASB).

Do not be surprised at the fiery ordeal among you, which comes upon you for your testing…but to the degree that you share the sufferings of Christ, keep on rejoicing, so that also at the revelation of His glory you may rejoice with exultation (1 Peter 4:12-13 NASB).

Consider it all joy, my brethren, when you encounter various trials, knowing that the testing of your faith produces endurance (James 1:2-3 NASB).

For those who are worried:

Be anxious for nothing, but in everything by prayer and supplication with thanksgiving let your requests be made known to God. And the peace of God, which surpasses all comprehension, will guard your hearts and your minds in Christ Jesus. Finally, brethren, whatever is true, whatever is honorable, whatever is right, whatever is pure, whatever is lovely, whatever is of good repute, if there is any excellence and if anything worthy of praise, dwell on these things. The things you have learned and received and heard and seen in me, practice these things; and the God of peace will be with you (Philippians 4:6-9 NASB).

Do not fret because of evildoers, be not envious toward wrongdoers (Psalm 37:1 NASB).

For those who feel oppressed and in distress:

Answer me when I call, O God of my righteousness! You have relieved me in my distress; be gracious to me and hear my prayer (Psalm 4:1 NASB).

My heart is in anguish within me, and the terrors of death have fallen upon me. Fear and trembling come upon me, and horror has overwhelmed me. I said, "Oh, that I had wings like dove! I would fly away and be at rest. Behold, I would wander far away, I would lodge in the wilderness. Selah. I would hasten to my place of refuge from the stormy wind and tempest"…I shall call upon God, and the LORD will save me. Evening and morning and at noon, I will complain and murmur, and He will hear my voice. He will redeem my soul in peace from the battle which is against me, for they are many who strive with me (Psalm 55:4-8, 16-18 NASB).

When I was in distress, I sought the Lord; at night I stretched out untiring hands, and I would not be comforted. I remembered you, God, and I groaned; I meditated, and my spirit grew faint. You kept my eyes from closing; I was too troubled to speak. I thought about the former days, the years of long ago; I remembered my songs in the night. My heart meditated…I will remember the deeds of the LORD; yes, I will remember your miracles of long ago. I will consider all your works and meditate on all your mighty deeds (Psalm 77:2-6, 11-12).

Do not fear, for I have redeemed you; I have called you by name; you are Mine! When you pass through the waters, I will be with you; and through the rivers, they will not overflow you. When you walk through fire, you will not be scorched. Nor will the flame burn you. For I am the LORD your God, the Holy One of Israel, your Savior (Isaiah 43:1-3 NASB).

For those who need God's forgiveness:

Who is a God like you, who pardons sin and forgives the transgression of the remnant of his inheritance? You do not stay angry forever but delight to show mercy. You will again have compassion on us; you will tread our sins underfoot and hurl all our iniquities into the depths of the sea (Micah 7:18-19).

I acknowledged my sin to you and did not cover up my iniquity. I said, "I will confess my transgressions to the LORD." And you forgave the guilt of my sin (Psalm 32:5).

How to Pray

Over the years I've had numerous people tell me, "The only reason I'm here today was the knowledge that there was one person praying for me. That kept me going and gave me hope even when I felt hopeless." As I mentioned, sometimes I asked people exactly what they wanted me to pray about and allowed them to direct me. On other occasions I'd say, "This is how I'm going to pray for you this week." There will be times when this is what keeps your friend going.

And if you're part of a prayer chain, remember to get permission from the person before contacting the chain about him. This is also a way of asking, "Who would you like to know about this?"

As you pray, be sure to rely on the Holy Spirit for how to pray. Allow Him to bring to mind, through your imagination, the direction needed. Too often we quickly pray with our own words. Our prayers may lack freshness because they reflect our own direction and not that of the Holy Spirit. It's as though we're uncomfortable with silence or we feel we must "sound right" so we rush in. Too often our quick words can block out what the Holy Spirit wants us to pray.

> The purpose of prayer is to bring your friend to God and His resources, and to ask God to help your friend.

Be careful in asking your hurting friend to pray aloud or with you. He may be angry at God or not have the words at this time. "Grief has a way of plundering our prayer life, leaving us feeling immobile and empty."[1]

How then do you pray for your friend? Don't be intrusive with prayer. Ask your friend if he would like you to pray with him or for him. And don't pray long. Keep it brief and sensitive. If you have the opportunity to pray for someone in the midst of deep difficulty, it's a privilege. I've seen some people pray because they either didn't know what to say or they were uncomfortable with silence. I've heard some pray in an attempt to fix or convict their friend evidenced by the words chosen. The purpose of prayer is to bring your friend to God and His resources, and to ask God to help your friend.

Here are some prayers you can share with a friend:

O God, you are the Ruler of the universe, to you we commit our lives and trust in you for all our needs.

We don't understand the reason for the problems that we've experienced, nor do we need to. Our intent is to fully trust and fully accept the gifts you give as necessary and beneficial for us. Teach us to be thankful even when our immediate reaction is fear and distrust. Help us to be strong in our faith, to see you, and in every circumstance to give thanks, as this is your will for our lives.

Finally, Father God, bring us at last into your presence where all will be known to us as it has been known to you from before the beginning of time. Amen. [2]

Lord, we feel so alone and abandoned. I know you are still beside us, but help us to be more aware of your presence and what you might be trying to teach us through this crisis.

Protect us, and protect our children. Help us to forgive and to learn to be content—even in times of trial and tribulation.

I know that you desire good for us. Please guide and direct our paths. Amen. [3]

O Lord, we have experienced a great tragedy and wrong. We are suffering and grieving over our pain and loss. Please help us. Please come and comfort us in our heartache and grief. Give us wisdom to know how to help one another through this crisis. Give us strength to do the practical things that are necessary. Give us discernment to help each other in our personal and corporate suffering. Give us renewed faith to trust in you. And give us hope that we may be vessels of your goodness and mercy as we wait upon you. Amen. [4]

What's the best way to pray with your friend? Let me share the five kinds of prayers during difficulty Dr. Gordon MacDonald suggested at a trauma conference in New York. [5] I've intermixed his basic outline with my comments and suggestions.

There are five kinds of prayers that your friends need as an intervention during their time of difficulty.

Give a *prayer of encouragement*. *Encourage* means to press courage into a person. *Discourage* means to suck the courage out of a person. Your hope, your courage, your belief in them and the future can be transferred to your friend. Ask for God to encourage your friend, to give him strength and courage. You might share with him how precious he is in God's sight. Read a Scripture such as Ephesians 1:4-6 to the person:

> Even before he made the world, God loved us and chose us in Christ to be holy and without fault in his eyes. God decided in advance to adopt us into his own family by bringing us to himself through Jesus Christ. This is what he wanted to do, and it gave him great pleasure. So we praise God for the glorious grace he has poured out on us who belong to his dear Son (TLB).

A prayer might be, "Oh God, my friend means so much to me and to you. I believe as you do that he has the ability and the strength to carry on in the midst of this difficulty. Give him a clear mind, a peaceful mind, and your guidance."

When a person questions whether or not God cares for him, I've shared portions of this song, an adaptation of Zephaniah 3:14 and 17 and Psalm 54:2 and 4.

> And the Father will dance over you in joy!
> He will take delight in whom He loves.
> Is that a choir I hear singing the praises of God?
> No, the Lord God Himself is exulting over you in song!
> And He will rejoice over you in song!
> My soul will make its boast in God,
> For He has answered all my cries.
> His faithfulness to me is as sure as the dawn of a new day.
> Awake my soul and sing!
> Let my spirit rejoice in God!
> Sing, O daughter of Zion, with all of your heart!
> Cast away fear for you have been restored!
> Put on the garment of praise as on a festival day.
> Join with the Father in glorious, jubilant song.
> God rejoices over you in song![6]

A prayer you could share might be:

> Dear God, thank You for Your act of choosing, adopting, and making my friend Your heir. Thank You that he is never out of Your mind. Thank You for the never-ending joy You have over him. May he experience all of this at this moment in time.

Another prayer is the *prayer of restoration.* This is for the person who has failed or thinks he's failed. He has nothing left and is exhausted. Grief has overwhelmed him. He needs someone to pray and help restore a sense of grace in his life. And he needs this often. His tank is empty, and it needs to be filled. Perhaps it can be as simple as, "Lord, fill my friend with hope for today and tomorrow. May he be secure in Your arms" or "Lord, help my friend know he is loved."

Gordon MacDonald prayed for a friend in this way:

> O Lord God, here's my friend whom I've come to love. You know how much he's hurting today. Lord, I know that he's fearful. I know that he's in physical pain. Lord, he needs something from you that no human being can give him. He needs to know that tomorrow can be brighter than anything that's been in the past. Lord, he needs the kind of strength that only heaven can give. So, Lord, would you take my friend today? I put my hands on him so you know who he is. Would you take my friend today and bring healing to his broken life.[7]

A third kind of prayer is the *prayer of affirmation.* That's the prayer in which you recognize something in your friend that he can't see in himself.

> Lord, I thank You for the way my friend is making such good decisions this past week and the way he continues to do so. We see what You are doing in his life.

When you pray a prayer of affirmation for your friend, when you pray before the Lord on behalf of your friend, you are helping build the value and confidence that God wants him to have. In doing this, you're a "balcony person." You're leaning out of the balcony and saying, "Yes, you can do it! You're capable. See what you've already done. Wow!" You affirm through your comments and your prayers.

There is also a *prayer of blessing*, in which you pronounce upon another person what you know is God's purpose and will for him. This is also verbally invoking God's gracious power in your friend's life. You find this being done within the Scriptures again and again:

> The LORD bless you and keep you; the LORD make his face shine on you and be gracious to you; the LORD turn his face toward you and give you peace (Numbers 6:24-26).

What could you say to do this?

> Blessed be the God and Father of our Lord Jesus Christ. May He bless you with…

> May the Lord bless you and keep you strong…

> May the Lord give you hope that will neither cause despair nor disappoint…

Last is the *prayer of intercession*. This is called for when your friend is so weak and needy that you need to stand between him and God and pray on his behalf. In John 17 we read about Jesus interceding for His disciples. We too are called to pray on our friend's behalf. You will know what your friend needs as you listen to what he says to you. You might pray something like this:

> Lord Jesus, I pray the very words and thoughts of God for the protection of my friend. Please honor my prayers and surround my friend with Your protection. Protect him from all evil. In the name of Jesus, I ask. Amen.

> Father, sometimes events intrude into our lives that bring distress and discouragement. Use Your Word and the work of Your Holy Spirit to lift this burden from my friend and

bring comfort. I thank You in advance for doing this. In Jesus' name, I pray. Amen.

Dear God, my friend needs the Holy Spirit as the Great Comforter at this moment to overcome the pain and distress.

Be simple in your prayers. Be short. Be sincere. And if you promise to pray, write yourself a reminder so you are faithful to follow-through. Let your friend know you've been praying. You'll never fully understand the power of prayer in your hurting friend's life, but you can sure it's making an impact.[8]

Chapter 13

What to Do and What Not to Do

I would like to help. I really would. But I just don't know what to say. I'm sure I say too much, and sometimes I think what I say hurts more than it helps. So most of the time I stay away and don't do anything at all." Can you relate?

One of your friends might come to you with a problem you've never encountered before. You wonder, *What should I say? How should I respond?* As Christians, we are given opportunities to share Christ's love by the way we reach out to comfort and support others when they've endured a loss. But there are also healthy guidelines for us to follow when interacting with a grieving or troubled friend or relative. A number of suggestions have already been given throughout this book. Some will be reiterated here because they are so important, but there will be some new guidelines discussed as well.

The "Do Nots"

Four major "do nots" need to be followed:

- Do not withdraw from the relative or friend.
- Do not compare, evaluate, or judge the person or her responses.
- Do not look for sympathy for yourself.
- Do not patronize or pity the person.

Do not withdraw. In the case of any loss, a person needs continuing, ongoing support from a number of people. Often the support we give is out of proportion to what the person needs. When there is a death, the bereaved friend is often inundated by people, calls, and cards right away. But two weeks later, when the sorrow and loss is really starting to be felt, she feels like a social outcast. Nobody calls and nobody writes. One woman remarked, "Few people call now. I'm very lonely. No one worries about my meals or how I am managing my time. People suddenly disappeared, assuming I'm fully recovered from my loss. I'm not recovered. My loneliness now seems even worse. I'm embarrassed that I miss feeling special."[1]

It's as though the whole world has gone merrily on its way, leaving the person alone. This creates a tremendous feeling of isolation. The bereaved individual needs comfort on a consistent basis. She needs to be able to talk about what has occurred and to reminisce. For example, in both death and divorce there are major decisions that need to be made. In all types of loss a support group may be needed immediately.

Do not compare. When you see your friend or relative, the first and most basic response is to ask how she is doing and feeling. A simple "How are you doing? It's been ten days since you lost your mother. How are you feeling?" will open the door to conversation and support. The important thing then is to let the person talk without feeling that you're comparing, evaluating, or judging her responses, her grieving process, or her decisions.

Do not look for sympathy for yourself. This third "do not" may sound strange to you, but it does happen. Some people talk more about their own sense of loss and grief (current or in the past) in an effort to express their sorrow and empathy. But the other person isn't in the best position to offer support or dig out the subtle message the people are trying to send. This is a time for friends to give, not receive. If you need assistance, get it from somebody else for now.

Do not patronize. Have you felt looked down upon or that the other person thinks you don't measure up to her standards or responses? You know what that feels like, don't you? You feel dependent and childlike.

You wallow in self-pity and feel worse than before you interacted with the "helpful" person. Any kind of condescending response or behavior tends to reinforce hurt and adds another layer of inadequacies. Patronizing and pity basically show that we really don't care as much as we say.

"The Do's"

There are several positive guidelines to follow when ministering to a friend, relative, or neighbor. The first step is simply accepting what has happened and how he is responding. You may have your own perspective as to what your friend should be doing or how he should be responding, but you are not an authority on him, so you will need to suspend your expectations.

Accept him and let him know his feelings are normal. Some are going to apologize to you for their tears, their depression, or their anger. You'll hear comments like, "I can't believe I'm still crying like this. I'm so sorry" or "I don't know why I'm so upset even though it was unfair letting me go like that. And after fifteen years at that job. I know I shouldn't be angry, but I guess I really am."

You can be an encourager by accepting his feelings and the fact that he has them. Give him the gift of letting him face his feelings and expressing them. There are many statements you can make to this friend:

> "I don't want you to worry about crying in front of me. It's hard to feel this sad and not express it in tears. You may find me crying with you at times."

> "I hope you feel the freedom to express your sorrow through tears in front of me. I won't be embarrassed or upset. I just want to be here with you."

> "If I didn't see you cry, I'd be more concerned. Your crying tells me you are handling this in a healthy way."

> "If I had experienced what you've been through, I would

feel like opening my eyes and letting the flood of tears come pouring out. Do you ever feel like that?"

Anger is another feeling that is difficult for many people to express. You can use comments like these:

> "It's natural to feel anger and hostility toward everyone and everything that had to do with your wife's death. I feel angry too."

> "You must be very angry that your baby has suffered, and you can't do anything about it."

> "It's normal and reasonable to be angry and resentful when you've lost your baby while others have healthy ones."

> "You've lost your daughter. You have a right to be angry and frustrated."

> "It must be hard to find the words to express your anger, helplessness, and frustration right now."

> "It's important that you allow yourself to express your anger and rage—no matter how much others try to discourage you."[2]

Your encouragement for him to express his feelings will help him understand that you're not going to withdraw from him. Reassure him that you're not going to leave because of his feelings or that you're not going to try to talk him out of feeling the way he does. Your support is going to remain constant.

Another positive way of responding is with touch, but be sensitive to the person you're ministering to. He may not be as comfortable with touch as you are. If he seems to reject your physical gestures, such as hugs or a hand on the shoulder, be sure to respect his space. If you extend a hand and he stiffens up, it's a good indication that your brief words and physical presence will help more than touch. In time he may come to you and say, "I need a hug."

Sometimes it helps just to say, "I'll be here in the house with you for a while. When you need me to leave or I can do something for you, please let me know." Never assume he doesn't need you. Find out by talking with him.

Many people you minister to *will* need touch, since for many people touching eases the emptiness of the inner pain. A widow expressed her feelings in this way:

> Your mind is still on crutches...There is something awe-inspiring, silencing, and shattering about emotional pain that does leave one at a loss for words. Perhaps gestures are better. I've mentioned before my need for hugs. I'm sure other people feel the same way. Human physical comfort, no strings. I saw a cartoon once, no caption...It was [on a] vending machine; the sign on it read: "Hugs 25 cents." I wish I could have one installed. [3]

In his delightful book *Just a Touch of Nearness*, Fred Bauer tells this story:

> I once heard about the tragic traffic death of a young child. Nancy, just six years old, had been struck by a speeding car. Her parents were devastated. So were her schoolmates, especially Joyce, Nancy's closest friend. As soon as Joyce heard the news about Nancy; she wanted to run to her friend's house. But Joyce's mother thought it would be too upsetting for their daughter and for Nancy's parents. "Daddy and you and I will go to the funeral," she consoled. "You can see Nancy's parents there." But a tearful Joyce insisted that she must see them immediately.
>
> What worried Joyce's mother was what she herself might say to the grieving parents. But finally, reluctantly, she agreed to take her daughter to Nancy's house. And when they arrived, Joyce ran to her lost friend's mother, climbed upon her lap, and threw her arms around her. Wordlessly the two of them cried out their mutual hurt.

No one who came to say "I'm sorry" said it better than Joyce.[4]

The Gift of Listening

One of the greatest gifts you can give to a hurting, grieving person is the gift of listening, as we've already talked about. When people know you hear them, they will trust you and feel safe with you. And if you are a good listener, they will be more apt to invite you into their lives. Those you listen to will also learn through your example to respond openly and lovingly to what you share with them.

Some people will be attacked by the "if onlys." They feel guilty or ashamed they didn't help, even though they had no responsibility in the matter or couldn't have done anything about what happened. Let your friend share with you, and then gently help her identify if her statements are "if only" and "regret" related. To open up more discussion, you can make statements like these:

> "What could you really have done to prevent that from happening?"

> "Would that really have been possible?"

> "Are there others who could have done anything? If so, why didn't they?"

> "I can see how you might feel that way, but there really was nothing any of us could have done."

Above all, don't say too much to the hurting person. Your presence speaks volumes. Joseph Bayly wrote a book many years ago called *The Last Thing We Talked About*. It's the story of how he and his wife coped with the death of three of their sons. He gave this advice:

> Sensitivity in the presence of grief should usually make us more silent, more listening. "I'm sorry" is honest; "I know how you feel" is usually not—even though you may have experienced the death of a person who had the same

familial relationship to you as the deceased person had to the grieving one. If the person feels that you can understand, he'll tell you. Then you may want to share your honest, not prettied-up feelings in your personal aftermath with death. Don't try to "prove" anything to a survivor. An arm around the shoulder, a firm grip of the hand, a kiss: these are the proofs grief needs to logical reasoning. I was sitting, torn by grief. Someone came and talked to me of God's dealings, of why it happened, of hope beyond the grave. He talked constantly; he said things I knew were true. I was unmoved except to wish he would go away. He finally did. Another came and sat beside me. He didn't ask leading questions. He just sat beside me for an hour and more, listened when I said something, answered briefly, prayed simply, left. I was moved. I was comforted. I hated to see him go. [5]

Patience: A Necessary Character Quality

If there is one character quality that is necessary in ministering to a grieving person, it is patience. You will hear the same story, same details, and see tears over the same thing again and again. This is normal for the grieving person. It's even necessary. What may be quite uncomfortable for you is his anger. The extent of the person's anger may cause you to want to say, "Enough!" but anger is a natural, healthy response as long as it's within reasonable bounds.

You may even become a target for your friend's anger. If he withdraws, don't push him. This is part of grief. It's as though he moves in and out of the real world. He will progress at his pace, not yours. The author of *Beyond Grief* describes the process so well:

> No schedule exists for healing. A survivor is raw with grief and must endure much pain before healing takes place. The only course you can take is to avoid appearing restless or annoyed with the survivor.
>
> It may be difficult for you to achieve a balance between *acknowledging the loss* that caused the survivor pain, and

maintaining proper perspective in the face of that loss. You cannot help the survivor by blocking reality or steering a survivor away from painful reminders of the loss, but at the same time, you need to maintain a positive perspective while facilitating grief. You can do this by validating the person who died, talking about how the person touched or enriched the lives of other people when the opportunity arises, mention facets of life in which those activities or people who gave the survivor enjoyment. Keep the spark of those natural interests alive or at least present by mentioning them—the garden, the pets, the survivor's favorite shopping area, golf partner, or community interest. By doing this you are indicating to the survivor that *there has been a past* and *there will be a future* with these same things, people and place in it.[6]

Practical Help

There are also many practical things you can do to help, regardless of the type of loss. I hope you will begin to recognize and respond to the different types of losses people experience, some of which don't get much social recognition or support. Any major loss cuts deep, whether it is a divorce, personal rejection, job, or death.

With each loss you will need to (1) discover your friend's personal situation and needs; (2) decide what you're willing and able to do for her, realizing that you can neither do it all, nor should you; and (3) contact her and offer to do the most difficult of the jobs you've chosen. If your friend rejects your offer, suggest another. Specific tasks could include feeding pets, making and delivering meals, doing yard work, making difficult phone calls, obtaining needed information regarding support groups or new employment, providing transportation, being available to run errands, and so forth. At some point in time giving her a sensitive, supportive book on loss and grief could be helpful.[7]

If the loss affected one person, minister to that person. But if it affected the family unit, there needs to be a reaching out to each family member (adults and children). Be sensitive to *all* members of the family. I've heard many husbands say, "I'm so tired of people asking me how my wife is doing. For once I wish they'd ask how *I'm* doing." Discover which of their social involvements will be the most difficult for them and be available for support.

As the years go by, friends and relatives lose loved ones. Prior to Christmas, go through your card list to make sure you've made the needed changes so the name on the card doesn't upset the recipient. For a widow, receiving cards addressed to "Mr. and Mrs." may be painful.

Do's and Don'ts

What not to do: Don't minimize your friend's pain with comments like, "It's probably for the best," "Things could be worse," "You'll remarry," "You're young, you can always have another one," "You're strong, you'll get over it soon," or "You know God is in control." Comments like these might be attempts to offer hope, but to a hurting person they sound as though you don't comprehend the enormity of what's happened. They don't acknowledge the person's pain or loss.

What's best to do: You can offer simple, understanding statements, such as, "I feel for you during this difficult time," "This must be very hard for you," "I share your feelings of loss," and "I wish I could take the hurt away." Comments like these let the person know you acknowledge her pain and that it's okay to feel that way.

What not to do: Don't say, "I'm so sorry" as the end of your sentiment. Your hurting friend is probably sorry too, but he can't respond to that kind of comment.

What's best to do: Say, "I'm so sorry" and add, "I know how special he was to you," "I'll miss her also," "I want to help you and I'm available any time you need me," or "I've been praying for you. Is there something specific I should be praying for?" That gives the grieving person something specific and more satisfying to respond to.

What not to do: Don't say, "Is there anything I can do to help?"

What's best to do: Be aggressive with your willingness to help. Ask yourself, "What would I need if I were in a similar situation?" And then offer to do some of those things. You can also be specific. "I'm on my way to the store. What can I pick up for you?" "Would tomorrow be a good day to help you with the laundry?" "Would your children like to come over and play with my kids this afternoon?" Most of the time, a person in a crisis can't decide what she needs, so offering specifics helps. Besides, she probably doesn't want to impose so might be hesitant to bring up anything.

What not to do: Don't say, "You shouldn't feel that way."

What's best to do: Encourage your friend to keep a journal or write down her thoughts and feelings. Often just seeing her thoughts on paper will help her deal with what she's facing.

What not to do: Don't try to answer her questions of "Why"—"Why him?" "Why me?" "Why now?" "Why, God?" You don't have any answers at this time, and the true answer may not be apparent. Remember Job in the Bible? His friends didn't help when they visited. He told them, "You are miserable comforters, all of you!" (Job 16:2).

What's best to do: Simply respond to why questions this way: "I don't know why. I guess both of us would like to have some answers right now, especially you. I wish I had answers to give you."

What not to do: Don't offer spiritual advice regarding why she's facing this problem or tell her that she'll be a stronger person after going through this. We don't really know why tragedies happen or why some people have to go through so much trauma.

What's best to do: Agree when she expresses her feelings. When she says, "It's not fair!" Confirm what she's feeling. Say, "Yes, what happened to you doesn't seem fair, and it doesn't make much sense." Do this whether or not you share the same perspective.

What not to do: Don't put timetables on your hurting friend's recovery. Don't decide when she'll be ready for certain activities or emotions. When she doesn't fit into the timetable you've set, she may feel she isn't coping well or should be her old self by now. That only hinders real progress. Everyone is different and recovery times vary— sometimes greatly.

What's best to do: Allow your friend all the time *she* needs to deal effectively with the phases of her grief process.

What not to do: Don't quote Bible verses as a way to correct, minimize, or put your friend's feelings in a certain perspective. Saying "God will give you the strength" may seem impossible to her right now. Also, think very carefully before offering a passage. Make sure it can't be interpreted negatively. Grieving people tend to see the negative sides first. When you do offer encouragement, make sure it's heartfelt with the goal of comforting your friend.

What's best to do: Give spiritual encouragement from your heart. Include Bible verses that have comforted you at a difficult time, and let her know that. Also tell her you are praying for her daily. And when you pray with her, keep it brief and reflect her feelings in the prayer. Focus on how much God understands her pain and the fact that He wants to be her source of amazing comfort.

What not to do: Don't say "I understand" when you haven't faced the same situation. Also, telling someone that everything will be all right when you've never known the depth of her hardship is an empty statement. And you don't have any idea how this specific situation will turn out. And don't share horror stories of people you know who have been through something similar. She won't find that encouraging or hopeful.

What's best to do: Be honest about your experiences. If you haven't endured her particular kind of tragedy, say that: "I haven't been through what you're facing, but I want you to know I care about you and will support you through the difficult times ahead." If you've had a similar crisis, tell her about it briefly, adding that you can empathize with her. Realize that, of course, you can't *completely* understand what she's experiencing because you haven't been through what she has in the past that laid the foundation for her reaction.

What not to do: Don't ignore her needs after the immediate loss and hubbub has subsided. She still needs ongoing comfort.

What's best to do: Keep in touch for months, especially at the critical times discussed in this book, such as anniversaries. Let her know you're still praying for her. Ask how she's really doing and listen carefully. Send thoughtful notes with encouraging words.

What not to do: Don't expect unrealistic optimism or levity from your hurting friend.

What's best to do: Realize that her heart is full of pain and turmoil. Let her know that you are here to listen to her feelings and that you want to be part of the healing of that pain.

What not to do: Don't offer clichés or be unrealistically optimistic. Realize that those tendencies usually cover up your own insecurities and emotions. Dare to be real.

What's best to do: Indicate your love and support by saying, "I really feel awkward because I'm not sure what to say, what you need, or how to help you. But I do want you to know that I love you. I'm praying for you. And I'm available for anything you need help with."

What not to do: Don't use "should" or "if onlys" such as: "You should give the clothes away." "You should go back to work and get over this." "You should have more faith." "If only you had watched him more carefully." "If only you hadn't been so strict." "If only you ate better."

What's best to do: Allow hurting people to make the decisions and take the necessary steps to deal with the trauma. No one can tell another how they should feel.

What not to do: Don't offer unasked-for advice. If your suggestions weren't solicited they may not be appreciated.

What's best to do: Respond cautiously and prayerfully with uplifting and edifying ideas when your friend asks for your help. Let her know that you pray for her daily. On occasion, ask how she would like you to be praying for her.[8]

What not to do: Be careful in saying statements like "This must be God's will."

What's best to do: Let your friend know that God is present with her in this time of suffering even if she doesn't sense Him. Gently remind her that He is the Comforter and Protector in the midst of pain and tragedy. Be sensitive regarding how and when you share this so it won't come across as a cliché or platitude. As you walk through your own losses, you'll be better able to help others walk through their valleys of loss and pain. The walk can seem so lonely, but when people come alongside, just being there to listen, to weep, and to offer comfort, grievers are encouraged and sustained.

None of us walks alone. Jesus Christ experienced loss and pain, and He is with us all the time to sustain, encourage, and support us. Yes, life is full of losses, but He makes it possible to survive them, grow from them, conquer them, and move forward again.

Chapter 14

When to Make a Referral

Many of those who come to you will benefit from your help. But some will need to be referred to a counselor, pastor, or person with more expertise because of the severity of their difficulties or situations. Some of the best counsel you can give is to refer them to someone more suited to their needs. It's a sign of inner strength, security, and maturity to refer people without condemning yourself for lack of knowledge. Knowledge and acceptance of your abilities and spiritual gifts are essential. The apostle Paul said:

> Do nothing from factual motives [through contentiousness, strife, selfishness, or for unworthy ends] or prompted by conceit and empty arrogance. Instead, in the true spirit of humility (lowliness of mind) let each regard the others as better than and superior to himself [thinking more highly of one another than you do of yourselves]. Let each of you esteem and look upon and be concerned for not [merely] his own interests, but also each for the interests of others (Philippians 2:3-4 AMP, brackets in original).

Our training, experiences, and personalities are all variables that affect what happens in counseling. I make referrals to professional counselors, ministers, lawyers, medical specialists, financial specialists, or whomever I believe has the necessary expertise for my client.

Knowing When to Refer

One of the most common reasons to refer is when the person in crisis needs specialized assistance you aren't able to give with confidence. This doesn't necessarily mean your friend's need or problem is severe or radical, but it is one that you're not prepared to handle. Don't convey to the person that his problem is so serious that he's far beyond your help. That will increase his stress. Instead, let him know someone else will be able to help him more thoroughly and more specifically than you can at this time.

Another reason for referral is when there are indications of serious risk. Whenever a friend's well-being is at stake, ask yourself these questions: "Is he a danger to himself?" "Do I have the time and capability to assist him?" "Will this endanger my own well-being or other people?" If the answer is yes, referral to a professional therapist, such as a psychologist, psychiatrist, or marriage and family therapist, is necessary. In the case of a possible suicide in progress, get someone to call 9-1-1 for you. The emergency people can probably trace the call if necessary. If violence is involved, don't try to handle it yourself. Contact emergency services.

As the crisis situation that prompted a person to seek your help begins to lessen, you may want to refer if you believe long-term counseling for the problem or person would be helpful.

Finding Referral Sources

You can get personal recommendations from ministers, Christian doctors, Christian lawyers. Christian colleges, private Christian schools, and many seminaries are willing to provide referrals. Many communities have Christian businesses and professional directories that list therapists who profess to be Christians. Referrals to Christian therapists in your area may be obtained from:

- Focus on the Family, 8605 Explorer Drive, Colorado Springs, CO 80995; 1-800-A-Family (232-6459); http://www.focusonthefamily.com/lifechallenges/articles/consider_counseling.aspx

- American Association of Christian Counselors, 1639 Rustic Village, Forest, VA 24551; (800) 526-8673

Steps for Making Referrals

Do your homework. First of all, be sure you've done your homework by gathering all of the information your friend will need: location, hours, type of counseling, services offered, and financial policies.

The way you broach the subject of referral and handle this discussion will be very important for the referral to be successful. It's easy for your friend to interpret a referral as rejection or a negative judgment on the severity of the problem or herself. Your care and sensitivity need to be evident. A casual, relaxed approach is much better than leaning forward with a serious expression of deep concern. A statement such as, "I appreciate all that you've shared with me. It helps me know how much I'm able to assist and in what ways. I want to help you the best way possible. I believe I can help you the most at this time by recommending you contact a counselor with more experience working with these types of issues and situations. I have a list I can share of counselors with more training and expertise than I have in this area."

The person may accept this readily or may seem hesitant and puzzled. She may say, "You don't want to help me?"

"No," you should reply. "I *do* want to help you, and I may continue to see you from time to time. But I want you to get the best help available, and that is why I'm making this recommendation." She may reply, "But I've shared so much with you. It's difficult for me to share, and now you want me to go somewhere else and start over with a stranger? I want you to help me."

"I realize that it can be a bit scary to see someone else," you can say. "It took courage for you to share with me as openly as you have. I feel you still have the courage and capability to begin with someone who is better equipped to help you than I am. What can I do to make this choice easier for you?"

Help her make the choice. After you've offered your recommendations, the person has the choice of accepting or rejecting your suggestion of referral. The person needs to make her own decision. She needs to make the call so she'll follow-through. If she has a serious difficulty or problem, such as deep depression, physical difficulties, suicidal thoughts, abuse issues, an immediate referral is needed. You may have to insist gently by asking the person to trust your judgment. In a nonemergency situation, you can ask her to consider your suggestion and let you know what she decides. Be sure you let your friend know that she doesn't have to accept the referral to the specific people you mention just to please you. You may want to suggest two or three referral names if possible.

Follow up. Always see or call the person following her visit with the new source of help. Let her know you will continue to pray for her and that you're interested in her continued growth.

Notes

Chapter 1—Called to Help

1. Harold Ivan Smith, *When You Don't Know What to Say* (Kansas City, MO: Beacon Hill Press, 2002), 15.

2. Nina Herrmann Donnelley, *I Never Know What to Say* (New York: Ballantine Books, 1987), 21-22.

3. Ibid., adapted, 17-24.

4. Jerome Groopman, MD, *The Anatomy of Hope* (New York: Random House, 2004), 134-35.

5. Smith, *When You Don't Know What to Say*, 7.

Chapter 2—Don't Be a Miserable Comforter

1. Frederick Buechner, *Peculiar Treasures: A Biblical Who's Who* (New York: Harper & Row, 1979), 65.

2. Quoted in Bob Diets, *Life After Loss* (Tucson: Fisher Books, 1988), 148.

3. Charlotte E. Thompson, *Raising a Handicapped Child* (New York: Morrow, 1986), adapted, 38-41.

4. Mary Ann Froehlich and Peggy Sue Wells, *What to Do When You Don't Know What to Say* (Minneapolis: Bethany House, 2000), 98-99.

5. Ibid., 97-98.

6. Ibid., 96-97.

7. Ibid., adapted, 95.

8. Ibid., 94.

9. Betty Jane Wylie, *The Survival Guide for Widows* (New York: Ballantine Books, 1982), adapted, 115.

10. Michele McBride, *The Fire That Will Not Die* (Palm Springs: ETC Publications, 1979), 154, 147, ix.

11. "Seeing with God's Eyes," *Today's Christian Woman* (March/April 1986).

12. Alan Breslau, founder of the Phoenix Society, in a newsletter article published by the Phoenix Society, date unknown.

13. Erin Linn, *I Know Just How You Feel: Avoid the Clichés of Grief* (Cary, IL: Publisher's Mark, 1986), adapted, xii-xiii.

14. Rita Moran, *Compassionate Friends* newsletter.

Chapter 3—If You Want to Help, Listen

1. Drawn from communication studies done by Albert Mehrabian in the 1960s.

2. Harold Kushner, *Living a Life that Matters* (New York: Anchor Books, 2002), 123-24.

3. Leonard M. Zunin, MD, and Hilary Stanton Zunin, *The Art of Condolence* (New York: HarperCollins, 1991), 147.

4. Harold Ivan Smith, *When You Don't Know What to Say* (Kansas City, MO: Beacon Hill Press, 2002), 87.

5. William Barclay, *A Barclay Prayer Book* (London: SCM Press, Ltd., 1990), 344-45.

Chapter 4—Understanding What Your Friend Is Experiencing

1. Ronald W. Ramsay and Rene Noorbergen, *Living with Loss* (New York: William Morrow and Co., Inc., 1981), adapted, 47-48.

2. Therese A. Rando, *Grieving: How to Go On Living When Someone You Love Dies* (Lexington, MA: Lexington Books, 1988), adapted, 556-57.

3. Ibid., 44.

4. Carol Staudacher, *Beyond Grief* (Oakland, CA: New Harbinger Publications, 1987), adapted, 47.

5. Joanne T. Jozefowski *The Phoenix Phenomenon* (Northvale, NJ: Jason Aronson, Inc., 2001), 17.

6. Michael Leunig, *A Common Prayer* (New York: HarperCollins, 1991).

7. Therese A. Rando, *Treatment of Complicated Mourning* (Champaign, IL: Research Press, 1983), 512.

8. Glen W. Davidson, *Understanding Mourning* (Minneapolis: Augsburg Publishing House, 1984), 59.

9. Ibid., 59.

10. H. Norman Wright, *Will My Life Ever Be the Same?* (Eugene, OR: Harvest House, 2002), 100.

Chapter 5—Understanding a Friend in Crisis

1. H. Norman Wright, *Crisis Counseling* (Ventura, CA: Regal Books, 1993), ch. 1.

Chapter 6—Loss or Trauma?

1. Donald Meichenbaum, *A Clinical Handbook/Practical: Therapist for Assessing and Treating Adults with Post Traumatic Stress Disorder (PTSD)* (Waterloo, ON, Canada: Institute Press, 1994), adapted, 23.

2. Sandra L. Brown, *Counseling Victims of Violence* (Alexandria, VA: American Association for Counseling and Development, 1991), adapted, 9.

3. Diane Langberg, quoted from a presentation for the American Association of Christian Counselors (AACC) Training Conference, New York City, 2001, adapted.

4. Aphrodite Matsakis, *I Can't Get over It: A Handbook for Trauma Survivors* (Oakland, CA: New Harbinger, 1992), adapted, 6-7.

5. Ibid., adapted, 23-24.

6. Ibid., adapted, 10-13.

Chapter 7—The Hazards of Trauma

1. Diane Langberg, AACC Conference, Oct. 2001, adapted.

2. Sandra L. Brown, *Counseling Victims of Violence* (Alexandria, VA: American Association for Counseling and Development, 1991), adapted, 22-24.

3. Robert Hicks, *Failure to Scream* (Grand Rapids, MI: Baker, 1996), adapted, 46.

4. Raymond B. Flannery, Jr., *Post-Traumatic Stress Disorder* (New York: Crossroad, 1992), adapted, 36-37.

5. Terence Monmaney, "For Most Trauma Victims Life Is More Meaningful," *L.A. Times,* Sunday, Oct. 7, 2001, 9, citing research from Richard Tedeschi, University of North Carolina; Dr. Robert Ursano, Uniformed Services, University of the Health Sciences, Bethesda, MD; and Dr. Sandra Bloom.

6. Aphrodite Matsakis, *I Can't Get over It!* (Oakland, CA: New Harbinger, 1992), adapted, 134.

7. Ibid., adapted, 15, 153.

8. Ibid., adapted, 159.

9. Ibid., adapted, 160-63.

10. Ibid., adapted, 236.

11. H. Norman Wright, *Will My Life Ever Be the Same?* (Eugene, OR: Harvest House, 2002), adapted, chapter 8.

Chapter 8—Helping Your Friend

1. Karl A. Slaikeu, *Crisis Intervention: A Handbook for Practice and Research* (Boston: Allyn and Bacon, 1984), adapted, 89-90.

2. Ibid., adapted, 90-91.

Chapter 9—When Depression Hits

1. Richard F. Berg and Christine McCartney, *Depression and Integrated Life* (New York: Alta House, 1981), 27.

2. Mitch Golant, PhD, and Susan K. Golant, *What to Do When Someone You Love Is Depressed* (New York: Henry Holt and Co., 1996), adapted, 90-92.

3. H. Norman Wright, *Winning over Your Emotions* (Eugene, OR: Harvest House, 1998), adapted, 32-33.

4. Ibid., 36.

Chapter 10—Helping a Suicidal Friend

1. Judith Acosta and Judith Simon Prager, *The Worst Is Over* (San Diego: Jodere Group, 2002), 247.

2. *The National Newsletter for the Compassionate Friends* (Winter 1981), adapted.

3. Eric Marcus, *Why Suicide?* (San Francisco: Harper and Row, 1996), 164.

4. Ibid., 137.

5. Ibid., 139.

6. Harold Ivan Smith, *A Long-Shadowed Grief: Suicide and Its Afterlife* (Lanham, MD: Cowley Publications, 2007), 3-4, 26.

7. David B. Biebel and Suzanne L. Foster, *Finding Your Way After the Suicide of Someone You Love* (Grand Rapids, MI: Zondervan, 2005), 169.

Chapter 11—Say It in Writing

1. Leonard M. Zunin, MD, and Hilary Stanton Zunin, *The Art of Condolence* (New York: HarperCollins, 1991), adapted, 35-39.

2. Ibid., 38.

3. Robert V. Ozment, *When Sorrow Comes* (Waco, TX: Word Books, 1970), 50.

4. Barbara Russell Chesser, *Because You Care* (Waco, TX: Word Books, 1987), 119.

5. Norman Vincent Peale, *Wonderful Promises* (Carmel, NY: Guideposts, 1983), 32.

6. Phyllis Hobe, *Coping* (Carmel, NY: Guideposts, 1983), 233.

7. Zunin and Zunin, *Art of Condolence*, 61-62.

8. Ibid., 72-73.

9. Ibid., 97-98.

Chapter 12—Praying for Your Friend

1. J. Rupp, *Praying Our Goodbyes* (Notre Dame, IN: Ave Maria Press, 1988), 79.

2. Lisa Barnes Lampman, ed., *Helping a Neighbor in Crisis* (Wheaton, IL: Tyndale House, 1997), adapted, 67.

3. Ibid., 40.

4. Ibid., 68.

5. Gordon MacDonald, PhD, Trauma Conference, New York, 2001.

6. "And the Father Will Dance," lyrics adapted from Zephaniah 3:14 and 17 and Psalm 54:2, 4, arranged by Mark Hayes. Used by permission.

7. MacDonald, Trauma Conference, New York, 2001.

8. Ibid., adapted.

Chapter 13 —What to Do and What Not to Do

1. Judy Tatelbaum, *The Courage to Grieve* (New York: Harper & Row, 1980), 44.

2. Donna Ewy and Rodger Ewy, *Death of a Dream* (New York: Dutton, 1984), adapted, 80.

3. Betty Jane Wylie, *The Survival Guide for Widows* (New York: Ballantine Books, 1982), adapted, 80.

4. Fred Bauer, *Just a Touch of Nearness* (Norwalk, CT: C.R. Gibson Co., 1985), 24-25.

5. Joseph Bayly, *The Last Thing We Talked About* (Colorado Springs: Cook Communications, 1969, 1992), 40.

6. Carol Staudacher, *Beyond Grief* (Oakland, CA: New Harbinger Publications, 1987), 230-31.

7. Ibid., adapted, 231-32.

8. Lauren Briggs, *What You Can Say When You Don't Know What to Say* (Eugene, OR: Harvest House Publishers, 1985), adapted, 150-55.

Great Harvest House Books by
H. Norman Wright

101 Questions to Ask Before You Get Engaged

101 Questions to Ask Before You Get Remarried

101 Ways to Build a Stronger, More Exciting Marriage

After You Say "I Do"

After You Say "I Do" Devotional

Before You Remarry

Before You Say "I Do"®

Before You Say "I Do"® Devotional

Before You Say "I Do"™ DVD

Coping with Chronic Illness

Finding the Right One for You

*Helping Your Kids Deal with Anger, Fear,
and Sadness (ebook only)*

Quiet Times for Couples

Quiet Times for Every Parent (ebook only)

Quiet Times for Those Who Need Comfort (ebook only)

Reflections of a Grieving Spouse

Strong to the Core (Devotional, ebook only)

Success over Stress

Truly Devoted (Dogs)

Winning over Your Emotions

Quiet Times for Couples

*"Let Norman Wright guide you together to God...
and your marriage will never be the same."*
MAX LUCADO

**Uplifting, insightful devotions that will inspire,
encourage, and strengthen your marriage**

In these short devotions that promote togetherness, joy, and sharing your dreams, trusted Christian counselor and bestselling author Norm Wright offers...

- innovative ideas to establish and maintain a flourishing marriage
- insights for encouraging intimacy and harmony
- little and big things you can do to enhance your relationship
- specific suggestions for accommodating differences and handling conflicts
- great ideas for supporting and helping your spouse

Your relationship will become more loving, considerate, and united as the two of you experience these quiet "together times" filled with deep insights, powerful meditations, God's presence, and His truths and love.

Strong to the Core

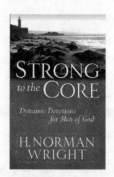

*Men, strengthen Your Heart, Mind, and Spirit
in Just 5 Minutes a Day!*

Bestselling author Norm Wright has a proven plan
to help you strengthen your core—your spiritual
life, your family life, and your personal life. In these short devotions you'll
find biblical truth, wisdom for growing your relationships, and time-
tested advice for handling temptations and working through problems.

Professional knowledge coupled with practical insights garnered through
Norm's many years as a respected Christian counselor will help you...

- increase your understanding of the Lord and His will
- communicate more effectively in relationships, especially
  marriage
- strengthen your reliance on God and His Word
- develop traits that reveal your heart for God
- implement your faith and God-given gifts to help others

Strong to the Core encourages you to embrace God's call to live for Him,
represent Him, and take a stand for Him. You can make a difference!

Success over Stress

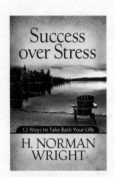

Isn't it time to take back your life?

You can't eliminate all stress, but you can certainly lessen its negative impact. Noted Christian counselor Norm Wright shares the action steps that have enabled thousands of people to find greater happiness, satisfaction, and peace. Through true, encouraging stories, biblical wisdom, and practical suggestions, you'll discover how to decrease your stressors by:

- simplifying your work and home life
- releasing any emotional baggage
- taking control of your schedule and finances
- establishing livable goals and priorities
- experiencing God's presence more fully

Packed with sound advice and proven steps for handling worry, fear, irritation, and more, *Success over Stress* reveals how you can experience more joy, energy, and satisfaction every day.

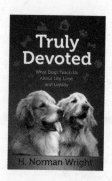

Truly Devoted

*What Dogs Teach Us About Life,
Love, and Loyalty*

Packed with dog adventures and antics that will make you smile, these devotions by trusted counselor Norm Wright provide warmhearted insights for improving your relationships with the people in your life. Drawing on wisdom from God's Word, many years of helping people, and time spent working with his beloved dogs, Norm encourages you to...

- explore how you can share God's faithfulness and comfort
- understand God through the world around you
- relax and enjoy the amazing love God offers
- meet with God every day
- draw strength, faith, and patience from His Word

As you glimpse some of the joys and quirks of four-legged family members, you'll discover surprising ideas that will help you draw closer to God, live vibrantly, and experience more fulfilling connections with family and friends.

To learn more about Harvest House books and
to read sample chapters, visit our website:

www.harvesthousepublishers.com

HARVEST HOUSE PUBLISHERS
EUGENE, OREGON